RON RUBIN

GOLD IN YOUR BACKYARD

VAL DE GRÂCE
BOOKS

RON RUBIN

GOLD IN YOUR BACKYARD

LESSONS IN LIFE, LEADERSHIP AND THE POWER OF A DREAM

All our dreams can come true—
if we have the courage to
pursue them.

■ WALT DISNEY ■

THE DEDICATION

I feel very blessed. As you will see in the pages ahead, I have had an exciting and deeply fulfilling life as an entrepreneur and business leader, and all along the way I have been guided and inspired by a wonderful array of mentors and advisers.

First among those mentors was my father, Hyman A. Rubin, a man whose good heart and common sense wisdom I will forever cherish. My dad urged me to go out and explore, to be bold and try new things, but his greatest advice for me was this: what you need to learn and the best people to help you are not off in some distant land. No. Often the real gold you want and need is right in your own backyard. And he was so right!

Dad, with joy and gratitude, I dedicate this book to YOU. And I do so with the hope that your wisdom and your uplifting spirit will inspire other entrepreneurs and business leaders to be bold, to go out and explore, to fearlessly build their dreams, but to always cherish the gold they have in their own backyards. ▪

From my heart,

RON RUBIN

RON RUBIN

▪

WITH PAUL CHUTKOW

TABLE OF CONTENTS

WISDOM
AND SPIRIT

The people who are crazy enough to
think they can change the world are
the ones who do.

■ STEVE JOBS ■

Find A Mentor

As I look back across my 50-plus years in business, and as I think about what I have learned along the way, I see 50 golden lessons that I want to share with you now, and the very first lesson is this: Find A Mentor.

Over the years, and through my reading, I have studied many of the giants of American business, from Sam Walton of Walmart and Sam's Club, to John C. Bogle, a legend in the world of finance and investment, to famed sports and business coaches like Nick Saban and Bill Campbell, and to Yvon Chouinard of Patagonia and Steve Jobs of Apple, and they all drove home to me the same essential lesson: no one builds business success alone. It always takes a team, it takes a culture of vision and commitment, of striving and resilience in both the good times and bad, and it always takes able mentors and advisers to help guide you on your way. As I said above, my dad was my first and most cherished mentor, and now let me tell you why.

My dad, Hyman A. Rubin, was born and raised in Decatur, Illinois, and in business and in life, he was rock solid. And family first. He was a child of The Great Depression, and he saw the breadlines, the unemployment, and the countless families thrown into misery. Then came World War II. Dad didn't talk much about those years, but growing up I could see how much he valued hard work, economic security, and the importance of taking good care of his family and the people at our company, Central Wholesale Liquor Co., headquartered in Mt. Vernon, Illinois.

My mom, Sylvia, was also born in Southern Illinois, in the tiny town of Anna. She and Dad met in the town of Cairo, Illinois, and they started our family right there. Later we moved to Mt. Vernon, Illinois, located south of Springfield and due east of St. Louis. My dad loved to cook. He had a special grill built in our backyard, where he loved to cook ribs for our family and friends, and later he developed a love for Chinese food. And Dad being Dad, he wasn't content to just go to Chinese restaurants. No, his guiding ethos was always Learn, Learn, Learn. So he went to work in a Chinese restaurant, to learn their art and skills first-hand, and later he converted our garage into a full-scale Chinese kitchen, with special equipment that he bought and had shipped in from San Francisco. Yes, that was my dad.

In 1972, when I finished college and joined the family business, the company was 22 years old, and my dad was especially proud of two major achievements: his company had no debt, none, and he had no personal debt either. That, I came to realize, was a lesson that came straight from the hardship years of The Great Depression. I worked side by side with my dad from 1972 to 1989, and along the way he taught me many golden lessons about how to succeed in business and in life, and I will be sharing those lessons with you in the pages ahead. But his first, most insistent lesson was always this: run your business and your personal life with one governing principle: No debt! No creditors at your throat!

Week after week I saw the virtue in that. If we needed a forklift, or a new truck, we would pay cash for it. Likewise, if we saw an intriguing new business opportunity, we would carefully evaluate the potential impact on our bottom line and on our vow to stay debt-free. As a result, everything we did was always clear and up front, and that gave us enormous freedom in the way we built our business. It also helped us maintain the confidence and trust of our suppliers, our customers, and our employees too. The lesson here was clear: in any business, your word is your bond and, as I saw first-hand, being debt-free helps build trust and solidify that sacred bond.

I also learned an enormous amount from another mentor, Frank Fourez Jr., who served as the sales manager of our distributorship. Frank was the best salesman I ever had the privilege to work with, and he was absolutely key to the way we built our business. And Frank instilled in me a lesson that was key to the success of our family business and to my later success with The Republic of Tea and the River Road Family Vineyards and Winery. And Frank's lesson was this: "Sell, Sell, Sell!" Frank taught me so much about the art of selling, about how to approach a customer, how to present our products, how to manage pricing, and how you might have the finest plant, the finest trucks, and the finest everything, but your success always depends on your ability to sell. What a crucial lesson that was! Looking back now, I feel so blessed to have learned all this from a man like Frank Fourez Jr. We worked together for 34 years, and no aspiring business leader could ask for more.

Then there was Julian B. Venezky. From day one of my father's liquor distribution company, Julian was his trusted partner, and they worked together and built the business on a magnificent foundation: a single handshake. No lawyers, no contracts, no complex revenue-sharing plans, no hidden obligations or agendas; everything was clear, up front, and far-sighted. Beautiful! A company built on trust. And what was the result? They started the company back in 1950, on a 50-50 basis, with my dad as general manager and Julian as his silent partner. And right from the start, they had a special understanding: when they started the company, Dad had something new in his life... me! At that stage, I was all of a year old, but Julian made my dad a promise: should the day come that I wanted to join the family business, Julian would sell his 50 percent share to my dad, to honor the trust and spirit with which they had started the company.

And so it was. In 1972, when I joined the business, Julian did sell his 50 percent share to my dad. But Julian stayed on as the chairman of our board, and I worked with him from 1972 to 2008. And we had a very special relationship: I called him "Uncle Julian," he called me "Brother," and over the 36 years we worked together, he always had his hand on my shoulder, guiding my way, and he gave me one piece of advice that I have cherished ever since. And I feel honored to share it with you now...

As Uncle Julian helped me understand, running a business is always challenging, it's always filled with risks, some you can anticipate and some you can't, but it is your job to manage all those risks to the best of your ability—and to learn the crucial lessons as you go forward. And one thing Uncle Julian taught me was this: in the face of an especially difficult issue or challenge, have confidence. Trust your mind. Trust your heart. And if I ever felt stuck or uncertain, Uncle Julian would always say, "Okay, Brother, take 24 hours. Step back. Take the time to put your thoughts in order, to see the situation clearly, then confidently make your decision."

Well, I would do that, but afterwards I can't tell you how many times I would still feel stymied, still unsure of how best to proceed, so I'd call up Uncle Julian and say, "Uncle, I still don't know what I should do! I just don't know!" And with that, Uncle Julian would come right back to me with advice that was pure gold: "You do know, Brother! You do know! Believe in yourself! Trust yourself! You have the answer waiting inside!" Yes! And as I soon came to realize, what Uncle Julian was really teaching me was this:

How to be a strong, confident, and very effective leader. The kind that charts a bold course and inspires others to come join the cause.

Today, when I see friends or business colleagues struggling with this problem or that, and not sure how to proceed, I often say to them, "You do know! You do know! Believe in yourself! Trust yourself!" And every time I offer that advice, and see the results, I bow in gratitude to my Uncle Julian, one of the finest mentors anyone could ever have. As you will see in the pages ahead, I had several other wonderful mentors, and they expanded my knowledge and reinforced what I had learned from my dad and Uncle Julian: Believe in yourself! Trust yourself! And Learn, Learn, Learn!

So, my first golden lesson for you is this: find your own mentors and advisors, men and women you can trust to share their wisdom and help guide you on your way. That's the best foundation you can possibly have! ∎

Read

I never got an MBA degree. I always wanted to, but instead I went straight into our family business. Once there, to learn as much as I could, and to be as helpful as I could, I created my own MBA program: reading as many business books as I possibly could. I even gave myself a specific goal: to read one business book every week. 52 books a year! This proved to be so enriching, and so satisfying, that I still read as much as I can.

The rewards from my reading have been huge. Competition in the business world is fierce, and rising to the top is never easy, but thanks to my reading I was constantly gaining fresh ideas and wider knowledge. And I absolutely loved the process! I devoured all sorts of business books, and I especially loved reading books about creators and entrepreneurs and how they had built their ideas into inspiring successes. To expand my horizons, every day I also read four or five newspapers and magazines, searching for wisdom, guidance, and essential life lessons.

With all this reading, I developed a life-long habit: I always read books with a yellow highlighter in my hand. I highlight those portions of the text that I find most important and inspiring, and that makes it easy to go back later and find the book's key passages. Given this practice, I don't like Kindles or other e-books; I like to hold a physical book in my hands, to feel its heft, and to fully appreciate the importance of what's inside.

Beyond business, I also love to read about adventurers, creators, and leaders of every stripe. And one day that brought me to Nick Saban, the legendary football coach at the University of Alabama. During his coaching years, Nick was a brilliant leader and team builder: his teams won seven national championships, the most in American history. So of course I had to read many of his speeches and his book, *How Good Do You Want To be? A Champion's Tips on How To Lead and Succeed in Work and in Life*. And through them all, Nick Saban brought me life and business lessons that I will forever cherish. For instance:

What does it take to succeed in football, in business, in medicine, or in any field you choose? Nick's advice was clear as crystal: To reach the top, in whatever you set out to do, you have to have a special passion, a special intensity, a special focus, and always, always, always you have to have an iron-like commitment to keep right on learning and growing. And when trouble comes, and you suffer the inevitable setbacks and hardships that life will throw in your path, you don't quit. Ever! Instead, you dig in, you learn the necessary lessons, and then you stand up and charge right back into action, stronger, wiser, and even more determined to reach the top. Yes!

To drive that message home, every year at the start of football season Nick Saban would share with his players this message: If you want to be happy for an hour, eat a steak. If you want to be happy for a day, go play golf. If you want to be happy for a week, go on a cruise. If you want to be happy for a month, go buy a new car. But if you want to be happy for your entire life, you need to find your passion, what you love to do, and then give it your all. Inspired by a sermon he had heard from Martin Luther King Jr., Nick would tell his players, "If you want to be a street-sweeper, don't aim just to be good at your job. Aim to be the best street-sweeper in the world! Aim to sweep the streets like Michelangelo painting the Sistine Chapel. Like Shakespeare writing great literature. Aim to have them post a sign outside your door saying, The greatest street-sweeper in the world lives here!"

Wow! Pure inspiration! No wonder his teams won seven national championships! Thank you, Nick Saban! That's the winning spirit!

To reach the top and become a champion does demand the right commitment and the right spirit. For sure. But it also demands more, much more, and here I was fortunate enough to discover a brilliant writer named Sally Jenkins. Sally was a Stanford grad, a sports writer for *The Washington Post*, a six-time winner of the AP's Sports Columnist of The Year Award, and in 2005 she became the first woman ever to be inducted into the National Sportswriters and Sportscasters Hall of Fame. Sally was, in sum, a giant in her field, and she wrote a book that was one of the most important I have ever read: *The Right Call, What Sports Teach Us About Work and Life*.

Sally's specialty was Leadership. Over the years, she followed the most successful teams, she observed and interviewed their coaches, and she tried to pinpoint the specific qualities that had made them so special as leaders and mentors. Then, in the opening pages of her book, Sally laid out what she had discovered and had come to understand: the greatest leaders, the ones who had built championship teams, had developed their own special process and also a clear path to follow, the path that had led their teams all the way to the top. And Sally called that path "The Road to Greatness."

The Road to Greatness. Perfect! Sally then set forth the seven stepping stones those coaches had used to advance their teams' progress along that Road to Greatness: Conditioning. Practice. Discipline. Candor. Failure. Intention. And Culture. Meaning the culture those coaches had fostered to train and motivate their players, and unify them behind a single, uplifting goal: to reach the top and become the very best they could be.

Bingo!

For me, this was it: Pure Gold. And, again, clear as crystal. Sally Jenkins had discovered and was sharing with her readers a proven formula and a proven pathway to success in sport. And with almost every sentence I read, I could see that her findings applied equally well to my own world, the world of entrepreneurship and business leadership. I could see a few more elements to add to her list, but the key elements were the same: Discipline. Practice. Resilience. Intention. And Culture. Yes, in my eyes, this was it: a clear map to follow, a map that all of us entrepreneurs and business leaders can use to advance our progress along our own Road to Greatness.

It took me a long time to absorb all this, years in fact, but finally it all snapped into focus. Nick Saban, with his book, had shown me the discipline, the commitment, the resilience, and, above all, the spirit it takes to become a champion. And Sally Jenkins, with her book, had shown me a clear, element- by-element process to build a winning team and carry it down that Road to Greatness. Thanks to Nick and Sally, now I could see it clearly:

What it takes to build success.

What it takes to build a dream. ▪

3

Take Risks

Now let me tell you a little story.

One day, back in 1985, when I had been working for my dad's liquor distribution company for 13 years, I spotted something new, an opportunity to expand our business across a much wider territory in Southern Illinois. In my eyes, this seemed to be a smart move to take.

At that stage, we were serving 36 counties, with about a million people in them, and the opportunity I saw would extend our network to eight more counties, serving an additional 1.5 million people. A big increase! To handle the expansion, we would need more people, more trucks, and lots more effort—and our success was by no means assured. Still, I was eager to jump right in. But my dad wasn't. In fact, he opposed the idea. Firmly. He was content with our position, and he saw no great advantage in expanding our payroll, our operating costs, and our daily and weekly workload. In sum, he felt, why rock the boat? Why take the risk?

Still, I was eager for more, eager for a fresh, energizing challenge, and I decided to press my case. At that stage, our company was run by a board of three directors: my dad, me, and my Uncle Julian. As I said that was Julian B. Venezky, my dad's trusted partner since the start of our business. When important matters came up, the three of us would convene a board meeting to examine the situation and weigh our options, and we did that again now regarding my proposed geographic expansion. As was our usual practice, at the end of our considerations we put the matter to a vote. It shocked my dad, but when we voted on it, Uncle Julian was on my side. Voting for the expansion. His spirit was positive, confident, *Let's go!*

Thanks to Uncle Julian's intervention and support, we turned our expansion into a strong and lasting business success. Indeed, my dad died four years later, in 1989, and I believe that if we had not taken the risk we did, we might not have survived as a small, family-owned business. The marketplace for wine and spirits is never easy, with big corporations always stepping in and looking for more reach and more control, but thanks to our expansion, our profits and our stature grew—and so did our confidence. I was pleased. And soon thereafter I spotted another opportunity, this time in an unknown and very uncertain realm for us: bottled waters.

Today, bottled waters are a staple of American life. But back in the '60s, '70s and early '80s, that was by no means the case. Upscale consumers, many with international experience, were drinking French bottled waters, like Evian and Perrier, but there was little country-wide demand for them. In the early 1980s, though, Perrier launched a very stylish PR and marketing campaign to expand their sales across America. Perrier's campaign clicked, and soon several U.S. companies were jumping into the game. And so was one start-up venture in British Columbia, a group called Clearly

Canadian. Their specialty, like Perrier's, was sparkling water, but to appeal to a much larger—and younger—audience they were featuring sparkling waters with touches of fruit flavor: mountain blackberry, wild cherry, orchard peach, summer strawberry, and the like.

I was impressed by the spirit and creativity of Clearly Canadian, and in 1990 I heard they were looking for quality distributors to help extend their reach in the U.S. market. *Bingo!* Could that be us? On the face of it, the idea was a bit crazy: we had no experience with bottled waters, none, but I could see a natural fit with our portfolio of other bottled beverages. Indeed, thanks to our recent expansion across Southern Illinois—and the added revenue and confidence it brought us—I could see us becoming a Clearly Canadian distributor for several states in America. But could I sell them on the idea?

Well, I did sell Clearly Canadian on the idea and we became not only distributors but also investors in their young enterprise. Talk about taking risks! I'm sure my dad would have formally declared us nuts, investing in a start-up venture in an iffy new market in America, but it all worked out well, even better than I had hoped. Indeed, by 1992, just two years after we jumped in, we had sold three million cases of Clearly Canadian. Three million cases! Not small potatoes! And not chump change either! So again our profits soared—and our confidence soared right along with them.

Then it happened.

Then I heard about a new book written by three entrepreneurs out in San Francisco: Mel Ziegler and his wife Patricia had created, from scratch, a prominent business success we all admired: Banana Republic. And now, with their friend Bill Rosenzweig, Mel and Patricia had moved into a new arena and launched something new and exciting, a premium tea company, The Republic of Tea, and they had written a book telling all about it from the inside: *The Republic of Tea, How An Idea Becomes a Business*. Wow!

What a tantalizing subject: How an idea becomes a business! As you can imagine, I rushed right out to buy the book—and I'm so glad I did!

Page after page, Mel and Patricia and Bill showed me how they had launched their idea and how they had infused it with a very special spirit. They had fashioned The Republic of Tea as a whimsical country, with their key people called "Ministers" and "Ambassadors," and their sales outlets referred to as "Embassies." Fun! And as I could see, Mel and Patricia and Bill had fostered a company culture of passion and excitement, reflecting the exuberant feel of San Francisco at the time—and I simply fell in love with their approach. This was business with a whole new sheen...

At that stage, The Republic of Tea was still just a start-up venture, and Mel and Patricia and Bill mentioned, almost in passing, that to really grow their business and extend its reach, they needed to find someone with experience in distributing bottled beverages. *Bingo!*

As soon as I read that, I thought, "Wow, that could be me!" So I reached out to Mel, Patricia and Bill and right away we clicked and joined forces. Exciting! And I loved it! And 22 months later, I threw all caution to the wind and took the biggest, riskiest gamble of my life: I bought The Republic of Tea! All of it! What a kick! What an opportunity! And it had all stemmed from my love of reading and from my confidence in taking risks.

In the personality tests that many companies use in their hiring practices, on a scale of 1 to 10, on issues measuring risk, I score about a 12! It's just in my blood. Still, not everyone enjoys or thrives on risk—in business or in life. But here is what I have learned over the years: if you want to succeed in business, and you're not by nature a risk-taker, that's fine. But then team up with someone who is! We all know people who love to climb mountains, race cars, go deep-sea diving, or start new businesses from scratch. My advice: Find them! Join forces with them! Learn how to harness their special energy and then see what dreams you can build together!

So what's the key here? Balance. In your business and your life, you need to find and maintain the right balance between taking risks and being overly cautious. And it pays—hugely!—to have mentors and advisors who can help you find the right balance. In this light, I will be forever grateful to my Uncle Julian and his positive, upbeat, *Let's go!* spirit. Without his wise intervention, I might never have gone on to build our businesses or live my dreams. So I say, straight from the heart, "Bless you, Uncle Julian! You believed in me, you inspired me, and I bow in gratitude!"

In the pages ahead, I will show you how I and my team took charge of The Republic of Tea and how we led it, step by step, down our own Road to Greatness. Before I do, though, I want to share with you another story, the story of an event that shocked me to the core and changed my life forever. And it was an event that brought me another lesson, a golden life lesson that I hope each of you will absorb, appreciate, and take straight to heart. ∎

Live Your Dream

Growing up in Southern Illinois, in the 1960s and early '70s, I was fortunate to be raised in a warm, loving family, in a peaceful community, and my father was running a very successful business. Life was good.

I was attending the University of Illinois, studying business, and my future path in life seemed nicely laid out before me. But then a friend of my father suggested that if I was going into our wholesale wine, beer, and liquor business, I should go out to California and study viticulture and enology at U.C. Davis, then, as now, America's premier program in the field. That would be ideal preparation for the day I joined the family business.

So it was that in the summer of 1971, when I was all of 22, I did drive out to California—and what an energizing shock that proved to be! This was my first taste of the magnificent wines and vineyards of the Napa Valley and neighboring Sonoma County.

And what a marvelous spirit was in the air! After the long years of Prohibition and its aftermath, the American wine industry was roaring back to life, with boundless optimism and a spirit of innovation, and right there my life's dream was born: to one day have my own winery, with sun-filled vineyards of my own, a place where I could devote myself, heart and soul, to the challenges and joys of making my own wines, and I'd do it right there in the heart of California Wine Country! Perfect!

Yes, that was it—my life's dream—and when I got back home that July, my parents asked me how it went and I said, "Great! I enrolled at U.C. Davis, I found an apartment, and I'm driving right back to California!" Mom and Dad were startled, of course, but they supported my decision. Starting that fall, I attended classes at U.C. Davis in the art and sciences of growing grapes and crafting fine wines, many taught by Professor Maynard A. Amerine, the most respected figure in the field. It was a fabulous year. And once back in Illinois, I joined my dad's business, but what I had learned and dreamt of in California was still racing through my veins. Two or three times a year, I would go back to California to meet with different wineries in the hope of becoming their distributor back in Illinois. I absolutely loved it! And there was an added benefit: I was able to bring new business to our company.

Now, fast forward to the age of 60. By then my parents had passed on, I was running The Republic of Tea, I was happily married to my beloved Pam, and I was the proud father of our daughter Julie and our son Todd. And they were both fine people, with a strong commitment to giving back and to leading lives of real meaning and purpose. In sum, my life was great! Except for one thing: I had yet to fulfill my ultimate life's dream, of growing grapes and making wines, in my own heavenly spot in California Wine Country.

Then it happened.

One morning, after a breakfast with Todd out in California, I suffered a "ventricular tachycardia"—a serious, life-threatening heart problem—and I needed to be flown by Medjet back to St. Louis for emergency heart surgery. What a shock all this was! I landed in the hospital on a Friday, the surgery was set for Monday, and the only thing I could think about was that my life might soon be over, that death might be just few heart beats away.

Even now, so many years later, I still remember lying in that hospital bed, at Barnes-Jewish Hospital in St, Louis, and facing the cold finality of death. And I remember my mind twisting and turning about what I had achieved in my life, what I had failed to achieve, and feeling absolutely horrible about the pain my death would cause to Pam and our kids, and to my teams and my partners in education and philanthropy. And here was the final blow: my great California dream would now be dead and buried too. Awful!

Well, fortune was smiling upon me. I had a first-rate team of doctors, and they opened my chest and installed an implantable cardio defibrillator, to regulate my heart and help manage any future episodes. The operation was a success. And when I finally got up from that hospital bed, I was filled with gratitude and with a whole new set of priorities to guide my life:

Live Your Dream! Don't wait! Do it now! Our time on this planet is limited, and we can never be sure what is going to happen tomorrow or even later today. So seize the day! Carpe diem! Build your dreams and do it now!

With that heightened awareness surging through my system, as soon as I had my strength back Pam and I set off to find our place in the California sun. We spent two years looking, and on December 20th, 2011, we finally had it, in Sonoma County, just outside the town of Sebastopol, a place of warmth and beauty, with exquisite landscapes and shimmering vineyards reaching up to the sky. Right there, with the stroke of a pen, our crowning dream came true, our River Road Family Vineyards and Winery was born, an event made all the sweeter by the terrible scare I had just endured.

Dear readers, today as I write, and as I count my blessings, my lesson for you here comes straight from my heart: The deepest satisfactions you will find in life will not come from the number of dollars you earn, or the number of bottles or boxes you've sold, or the number of magical places you were able to visit here or around the globe. No. The deepest satisfactions you will find will come from your family, from your spouses and children, from those who shared their love and supported your dreams. And it will come, too, from your friends and co-workers, from those who followed your lead, who joined your causes, and who stood faithfully beside you in the best of times and also the worst. Yes, that's where the true gold is, right in your backyard. So, my friends, in the end, when you step back and tally up your successes and your disappointments—as my heart scare forced me to do—count the many dreams you were able to build, yes, but also count the many hearts you were able to touch all along the way. ∎

PART TWO

INNOVATE!
EDUCATE!
INSPIRE!

Innovation distinguishes between a
leader and a follower.

▪ STEVE JOBS ▪

Innovate!

When I took the risk of buying The Republic of Tea, and going into heavy debt to do it, right away I was faced with several daunting challenges:

- How to build the company?
- How to build an exceptional brand?
- How to build a winning team devoted to our cause?

To meet those challenges, and build our company, I developed my own process, my own road, and it all began with a single word: "Innovate!"

At that stage, Innovation was not a natural part of my DNA. Far from it. My dad's company was a distributorship; we weren't creators, we distributed other people's brands of wines, beers, and liquors. In our field, we had a strong reputation, our business practices were tried and true, and during my two decades of learning and working closely with my dad, my Uncle Julian, and the rest of our team, I always felt I was on stable and very familiar ground. The Republic of Tea was a whole other story...

As I quickly discovered, Mel and Patricia Ziegler and their pal Bill Rosenzweig moved in a very different orbit. The "tried and true" had no appeal for them; they wanted to create something fresh and exciting. Still, when I bought it, The Republic of Tea was only 22 months old, it was still very much a start-up venture, and its future was far from guaranteed. So for the company to succeed—and to protect my substantial investment in it—I knew I had to expand my knowledge and thinking, and I had to develop a sound, reliable strategy for building the business. I also had to find new, creative ways to build our brand and have our products stand out boldly on store shelves. Daunting! And how in the heck could I do all that?

In my first year or so at the helm, feeling my way, I had no clear answers. Mel, Patricia and Bill were brilliant with design and packaging: thanks to them, we brought out our teas in stylish canisters, rather than flimsy paper boxes. We also offered our customers fancy new teapots from our "Minister of Enchantment," and we were experimenting with exotic new blends of tea, like "Ginger Peach," "Mango Ceylon," and "Vanilla Almond"—a far cry from the usual offerings from Lipton or Twinings. For me, with my roots in staid, traditional business, all this was charming, but when I went to the Fancy Food Shows, to showcase our products, people would ask me, "So, Ron, what's new? What new teas do you have coming out?" At a deeper level, their question really was this: "You're off to a fun start, sure, but how in the heck are you going to build your business?"

I wish I knew!

But then, slowly, the answers started to come, thanks in large part to my passion for reading. And two books really set me on fire. Back in 1985, the brilliant business writer Peter Drucker had produced a jewel: *Innovation and Entrepreneurship,* and in reading it I found the exact mindset I needed to embrace: "Innovate or Die!" Yes! Then there was Tom Peters, probably my favorite business writer of all time. With co-author Robert H. Waterman Jr., Peters had written a book I treasured: *In Search of Excel-*

lence, Lessons from America's Best-run Companies. The book is now considered one of the finest business books ever written, and for me it became an inspiring roadmap for how to build a successful, pioneering company. And from both Peter Drucker and Tom Peters the message I absorbed, down deep in my bones, was this: Don't stand on your laurels! Don't look to the past! Learn! Explore! Break free! Yes, Innovate or Die!

Creativity, of course, doesn't grow on trees, nor does Innovation. So right there, to build the future of The Republic of Tea, I knew I had to create a company culture that prized Creativity and Innovation, with a staff that felt empowered to generate bold new ideas, even in unexpected directions. For starters, I placed Innovation and Education front and center in our Mission Statement and in our budget—to make sure everyone understood exactly what we were after. As we stated it, with trumpets blaring, The Republic of Tea's mission was "to enrich people's lives through premium teas and herbs"—and to educate people about the many health benefits of our teas and herbs. In sum, we would let Lipton, Twinings, and the other reigning kings of the tea world stick with their usual offerings—Earl Grey, Irish Breakfast, Darjeeling, Chamomile and the rest—while we would break free and branch out in exciting new directions. And that is exactly what we did...

Early on, we promoted a fresh, galvanizing slogan: "Sip by sip, not gulp by gulp." Meaning our premium teas were to be savored as part of an enlightened lifestyle— not gulped down like a cheap cup of coffee. In line with that message and strategy, we featured our teas in specialty tea shops and upscale grocery stores—never a Costco or a Walmart. Likewise, we emphasized that our teas were grown in environmentally conscious ways, and we were also extremely health-conscious in our packaging and in our messaging. Our unique canisters, for instance, were air-tight, to ensure their freshness, and unlike traditional tea bags, ours came in round, unbleached tea bags, with no strings or staples attached. Very healthy. And soon we brought out the first teas in America to be certified by the USDA as "organic." And there was more to come, much more.

To support our message, and build our brand in ways that would appeal to new generations of tea consumers, each year we brought out fun new teas with tantalizing names and often with added health benefits too. For instance, we became the first company to bring out red "rooibos" teas from South Africa and pure 100 percent white teas from China. With all this, Creativity and Innovation soon became sealed in our company DNA, and so did Corporate Social Responsibility. In that vein, we joined hands with the Susan G. Komen Foundation, creating a "sip for the cure" line of teas that raised more than $1 million for the foundation's efforts to find a cure for breast cancer. And we formed a similar partnership to help find a cure for prostate cancer. These efforts were good for those causes—and good for our corporate image and spirit too. And, lucky us, we had results that were good for our bankers—and good for our hearts as well.

Naturally, then, I brought that same commitment to Innovation, Creativity and Corporate Social Responsibility to my next great venture, our River Road Family Vineyards and Winery. We were a young operation, producing only a few lines of quality wines, and those were the foundation of our business. We were intent on expanding our product line, of course, but we were also determined to do far more—for our company, our industry, and our environment. In sum, we set out to become a leader in the fields of sustainable agriculture, environmental protection, and social responsibility. And one primary objective here was to produce a better wine bottle, one that would be far healthier for the environment and much easier to recycle.

At that stage, some wine companies were bringing out their wines in cartons or plastic containers. But we were intent on finding a far better way. So we put everything under review: not just our wine bottles, but the way we harvest our grapes and move them through the production process, the way we bottle our wines, the way we construct our shipping boxes, the way we print our labels, and how we handle all of our recycling needs. This was a huge, costly, multi-level commitment. And what was the result?

In partnership with a specialized production house, Amcor Rigid Packing, we created a lightweight, Burgundy-shaped wine bottle made from 100 percent recyclable plastic, and coated with a thin glass-like lining called Plasmax, to protect the wine inside. Our Blue Bin bottles weigh just 52.8 grams, while traditional glass bottles weigh just over 400 grams—almost eight times as much! You can imagine how our Blue Bin bottles reduce shipping costs, facilitate recycling, and help protect our environment. We also created a special mobile bottling unit, to do all of our bottling on site.

And what was the result? Strong consumer approval. And community and industry acclaim. In 2016, the North Bay Business Journal named me Innovator of The Year. In 2023, the Sonoma County Winegrowers named us Sustainable Producer of The Year. And then in 2024, The Wine Economist, an influential wine industry blog, did an in-depth study of our new Blue Bin wines and bottles and then rendered its verdict: "Blue Bin wines are a big step in the right direction for wine innovation."

Wine innovation! Music to my ears! The long-term impact of our Blue Bin initiative remains unclear. And we're still learning. But this much I know: in the world of business, there are no guaranteed outcomes. But no business leader ever succeeds by sitting on their hands or refusing to seek a better way.

As you will see in the pages ahead, Innovation was not for us some small box to check on a long list of business do's and don'ts. No. Innovation was a leap of faith, an exciting plunge into the unknown, and it was just the beginning of a long and very difficult process to master. But our results have been fantastic. So what's the golden lesson here? What's my heartfelt advice for each of you? Think Big! Be Bold! Be Brave! Take risks! Innovate! And Learn, Learn, Learn every step of the way. Great results are sure to follow! ∎

Educate!

My dad never went to college. And I never earned an MBA. But our belief in the power and value of education runs deep inside our family's DNA, and we have made education central to our guiding mission and to so much of what we do at The Republic of Tea and at our River Road Family Vineyards and Winery.

At The Republic of Tea, for instance, we go to great lengths to teach our team, our partners, and our customers about the health benefits of our teas, and we even have a doctor who serves as our "Minister of Health," to help reinforce our teachings. At our River Road Family Vineyards and Winery, it's the same: we don't just sell fine wine. We teach our people and our customers about the environmentally sensitive ways that we enrich our soil, grow our grapes, craft our wines, and even bottle and ship them. And, as you will see, we have a distinguished Advisory Board that helps educate our teams and improve the quality of our work out in the fields and in our wine-making.

Every year, we also encourage our employees to commit themselves to 40 hours of continuing education, and we shoulder the costs. In a similar spirit, we established a special scholarship program, named in honor of my dad, and through it we have helped many of our team earn advanced degrees, including MBAs at Sonoma State University. We also support Sonoma State's Wine Business Institute, and I have had the honor of serving as the President of its Board of Directors, advising on its programs and how to expand its reach and influence.

Likewise, my commitment to education led me to teach in the MBA program at Saint Louis University, and it's why I created The Ron Rubin School for The Entrepreneur, at Culver Academies. The school is unique: it teaches the spirit and the fundamentals of entrepreneurship not to advanced MBA candidates, but to Culver's *high school* students. And The Ron Rubin School for The Entrepreneur does far more than that...

In a recent program, for instance, J.D. Uebler, the director of The Ron Rubin Entrepreneurship program, brought in a group of financial experts and business pros to teach a group of students how to manage their money and understand the essentials of financial planning. For the students, this was vital guidance and training. "Being financially literate is a life skill that demands attention," J.D. Uebler told them, "due to the harsh consequences of being financially illiterate." Other experts then advised the students on how best to save their money, finance the purchase of a car, and how best to manage their bank accounts, credit cards, and student loans. Terrific!

Alan Alderfer, a financial planner in Warsaw, Indiana, told the students—many of them seniors heading off to college—that after they graduated from university, they should continue to live modestly, as they had as students, and right away begin to pay off their college loans. At a time when the cost of college is so high, and interest rates are too, this was golden advice. How many high school kids get that kind of help? Not many! And that is exactly why I created The Ron Rubin School for the Entrepreneur, one of the most important and satisfying things I have ever done.

Throughout the pages ahead, you will see the importance that I and my entire family attach to education, not just for our companies, but for our wider commitment to our communities and our country. At our core, we believe that promoting quality education is absolutely essential to elevating the quality of life for all of us, and for assuring the future of this great country of ours. Our business focus may be premium teas and fine wines, but the lessons we cherish most are those that have a higher purpose, lessons that nourish our hearts and help our spirits soar! ■

7

Collaborate!

In my experience, many of the most successful entrepreneurs and business leaders have one surprising quality: Humility. The best I've met are not know-it-alls, not big shots who crave the limelight, and not those who are convinced they know all the secrets of success. Indeed, the finest leaders and entrepreneurs I've met are those who understand their limitations and seek out the specific help they need. And one sure way to do that: Collaborate!

I love collaborations. For me, collaborations are an ideal formula for business success: 1 plus 1 equals 3. Or much, much more! Also, in far too many businesses, leaders focus so tightly on their existing products and sales that they fall victim to tunnel vision, tuning everything else out of their thinking and practices. Collaboration breaks tunnel vision in a fast, very effective way: it forces you to see things in a fresh and much broader light.

At The Republic of Tea our first collaboration was with a fine foods company called Stonewall Kitchen, based in York, Maine. Their business was not tea; they created delicious jams, spreads, and baking mixes. At the annual Fancy Food Show, Stonewall often won awards for their products and that got me to thinking: might there be a way for us to join forces?

At the outset, I had no clear idea in mind, but one day I sat down with the owners of Stonewall Kitchen, looking for ways we might join forces. The owners of Stonewall were taken aback: "Come on, Ron, what have you got in mind?" Something fun, I replied: a marriage of your jam and our tea! And so it began: Collaboration. Brainstorming. Experimenting. Creating Together. And the result was something new and exciting: "Ginger Peach Tea Jam." Who had ever heard of such a thing? At that stage, no one!

Still, the Stonewall Kitchen team was very excited by our collaboration, as was our team, and soon we were dreaming of being selected by the Fancy Food Show as the outstanding new product of the year. How fabulous would that be! And guess what? First, our Ginger Peach Tea Jam was nominated as one of the outstanding new products of the year. And that was already a coup; it meant more clout and respect for both of our companies. Then came the actual awards ceremony, a high-profile event at the Javits Center in New York City and guess what? Right there our Ginger Peach Tea Jam was named the outstanding new product of the year! We were elated, of course, and for me this was tangible proof of the power of Innovation—and Collaboration.

From there, Collaboration became an essential part of our DNA and an essential step on our own Road to Greatness. My son Todd, who now runs The Republic of Tea, has done highly successful collaborations with Sony Pictures, Paramount, Disney and other film studios, even the producers of the hit British series Downton Abbey. Thanks to Todd, we even brought out a series of Star Wars teas. Yes, George Lucas, Luke Skywalker, Princess Lela—and us! The force was with us! And as these ventures have proved to us, time and again, Innovation and Collaboration go hand-in-hand. And they always bring us fresh ideas and fresh energy too. Who could ask for more? ▪

PART THREE

LISTEN AND LEARN

To build your business, hire the best,
most creative minds you can find—
then listen and learn as they teach
and guide you on your way.

▪ RON RUBIN ▪

Strategic Planning

I have to laugh.

When I took the leap and bought The Republic of Tea, I was really jumping into unknown waters. I was new to the world of premium teas, I was new to the world of entrepreneurship, and despite all the business books I had read, I had not found one reliable, step-by-step guide on how to take a raw idea and turn it into a lasting business success. More than once, I found myself thinking, "Ron, you crazy guy, what the heck have you done?"

Still, I trusted my gut, and I followed my dad's creed: Learn, Learn, Learn. And, lucky me, I found a series of advisers who gave me a whole set of new tools to use in building our company. Starting with Strategic Planning.

What the heck is Strategic Planning? When I started out in business, working alongside my dad, I had no clue. But every year Dad and I made a point of attending the annual convention of the Wine and Spirits Wholesalers of America, the WSWA. These were monster events, often attracting 3,000 visitors or more, and representing companies from all across the country. And every year, the WSWA featured special learning sessions, highlighting different ways to improve our performance in the wine and spirits industry. Those sessions were not always scintillating or worth the time. But one year, as I looked over the list of scheduled sessions, one did catch my eye. The speaker was a woman from Chicago named Barbara Shomaker. And her topic was Strategic Planning. I decided to go...

Well, Barbara was fantastic. In a smart, well-organized presentation, she showed us the multiple benefits of long-term thinking and long-term planning. Her message was clear as crystal: Don't think short-term! Think and plan three years in advance! Five years in advance! Define your goals! Then establish a clear roadmap to achieve those goals, with specific steps and specific target dates to guide your way and measure your progress. Barbara didn't use Sally Jenkins' specific terminology, and I certainly didn't make the connection at the time, but what Barbara Shomaker was really giving us was a process to help us move confidently down our own Road to Greatness.

Strategic Planning made perfect sense to me, and when I left Barbara's session I was determined to apply this knowledge to the way we ran our company. But my dad wasn't buying it. Old school as he was, his immediate reaction was: "Strategic Planning? We don't need Strategic Planning!" Still, Dad listened to me, and soon we invited Barbara to come teach us her process. From her office in Chicago, Barbara came down to our headquarters in Mt. Vernon, Illinois, and she helped us put together our first Strategic Plan. The results were impressive. So impressive that when I later made the leap and bought The Republic of Tea, I invited Barbara to come evaluate our strengths and weaknesses and help us chart our future course.

Barbara agreed to help us, and before we started I assumed we would do a three-year Strategic Plan, as we had done for my dad's company. But Barbara looked everything over and said, "Ron, The Republic of Tea is only 22 months old. We're not going to do a three-year plan; we're going to do a six-month plan! Let's get those six months right, then we can graduate to 12 months, and then 18, and after that we can start doing three-year plans." Wow! I was impressed! This was hands-on business wisdom that I would probably never get even from America's finest MBA programs.

Barbara Shomaker and I wound up working together for almost 30 years, until she retired, and her guidance was always invaluable, at so many levels. As she helped me understand, your Strategic Plan is your playbook: it sets your goals, your plan of attack, and how best to maximize your assets and move steadily down that road to success. Looking back now, almost 40 years later, I see my work with Barbara as a landmark step in my growth as an entrepreneur, first with dad's company, then with The Republic of Tea, and later, too, with our River Road Family Vineyards and Winery.

Today, my son Todd, our third generation in American business, continues to use Strategic Planning at The Republic of Tea, as I do at our River Road winery. And I still love the process. We usually go off-site for two or three days to define the precise goals we want to achieve—near and long term—and then we develop a step-by-step process to achieve those goals. And the results are always positive and uplifting. Bless you, Barbara! ■

9

Set Goals

As Barbara Shomaker taught us, the key to any Strategic Plan is setting clear goals and a clear timeline for reaching them. But as Barbara also taught us, don't set goals that are static or too easy to reach. That is not a formula for building confidence or improving your performance. Instead, we need goals that are constantly evolving, constantly pushing us to do better, goals that will lift our spirits—and our results. Let me drive that lesson home with an example that doesn't come from the world of business.

I've always loved to run. It's fun, it's exhilarating, it's challenging. And one day I said to myself, "Okay, Ron, it's time to go to the next level. It's time to run a marathon." This was a daunting challenge, trying to get strong enough to run a punishing 26 miles and 385 yards, but I was determined to give it a shot. But how to do it? You know how I rely on books for guidance. So, for starters, I spent a full month reading about how to run a marathon, how to train for a marathon, and about how to prepare psychologically for the challenge. From my reading, I developed a 26-week program that would get me into the shape I needed, with specific goals to mark my progress. I had never committed myself to anything as physically demanding as this—a full half-year of intensive training—but now I was on my way...

Talk about tough! My program had me run five days a week, with one very long run per week. In the beginning, I struggled, but week by week I was able to build my endurance—and build my confidence too. By the end of that half-year of training, I was ready to run my first marathon. I was nervous, yes, but those 26 miles and 385 yards sailed under my feet, and when I finished, I set no world record, but my feeling of accomplishment was fabulous—and my heightened confidence carried over into everything else I set out to do. And in the end, the entire experience reinforced what I had learned from Barbara Shomaker: Think big! Set big goals! But then develop a plan with smaller steps to reach along the way, and with target dates to measure your progress.

I have followed that formula in many different arenas. For example, with The Republic of Tea, and with my dad's example ringing in my ear, we set ourselves the goal of becoming debt free. So we developed a step-by-step plan, with clear goals and target dates to reach all along the way. Then I had a bigger dream: to share what I was learning with young people entering the world of business. So I set goals. I studied. I made the key connections. And soon I was teaching an MBA class in the John Cook School of Business at Saint Louis University. And that became another very satisfying thing to do.

Later, I applied this same formula when we launched our River Road Family Winery in Sonoma County and began crafting our wines. When we bought the property, it was producing only 25,000 cases of wine a year. So I set us an ambitious goal: to quadruple our output! And, yes, we did it: we're now producing 100,000 cases a year, with much higher quality wines as well. Then I set ourselves a bigger and far more complicated goal: to fulfill all the rigorous standards required to be declared a Certified B Corporation. As I will elaborate later on, this was a very important goal, with a purpose reaching far beyond the wine industry. But after 651 days of determined effort, we were able to reach that goal too. Hallelujah!

To sum up: Think Big! Set Big Goals! Then create your Strategic Plan, a map to follow, with clear steps and clear target dates to guide and inspire you along the way. As I can attest, those big goals and that clear roadmap will keep you excited. They will keep you focused. They will keep you pushing ahead, with all your juices flowing. And with each new goal you reach, your expertise will deepen and your confidence will grow. Do all this, dear reader, and I'm sure that one day you'll feel just as I felt the moment I crossed the finishing line of my very first marathon: "Wow! I really did it!" ∎

Public Relations

I love public relations!

When I bought The Republic of Tea, and had to rapidly build the business, I saw two roads to choose from: Public Relations or Advertising. Well, I've long been a believer in spending your money on PR to get press attention and build sales, rather than spending on advertising, and I held to that belief with The Republic of Tea and later with The River Road Family Vineyards and Winery too. And I still favor Public Relations.

That said, what is the secret for making PR work for your company? To answer that, let me share with you how we used PR to build our image and sales with The Republic of Tea. When I first bought the company and I examined what we could afford to spend on PR, I had a shock: we had to limit our PR budget for the entire year to just $24,000! Meaning just $2,000 a month! How in the heck could we make that tiny sum work?

Well, I found a very eager PR firm in St. Louis and I gave them tangible incentives to succeed. "Listen," I said, "to start, I can offer you a monthly retainer of only $2,000. Not much, but I promise you this: as we grow, you'll grow!" And it happened just that way. Pretty soon, as our sales and our image grew, our PR budget jumped to about $5,000 a month, and our agency's retainer jumped right along with it. The process was working.

Soon, as we learned how to use PR in the premium tea business, and we saw our earnings jump, I took another big step: I decided to hire a full-time PR specialist to run all of our campaigns in-house. Well, we found the right candidate, and we gave her a job title that made everyone smile: Minister of Enlightenment! Her job, after all, was to enlighten our staff about how best to use the power of PR—and to enlighten consumers and the marketplace as to how special we are. Missions accomplished!

Our success with PR at The Republic of Tea reinforced my belief in the power of Public Relations. Today at our River Road Family Vineyards and Winery we handle most of our PR needs in-house, but when we launch new products, and we need to improve our reach and impact, we hire outside PR agencies, often major agencies with offices in New York or Los Angeles. And what has been the result? Well, in my offices I now have piles and piles of positive articles from prominent publications like Time Magazine, Forbes, The New York Times, and from prominent food journals and blogs as well. In fact, I now receive a flood of positive articles and media mentions every single week—without spending a single dime on advertising! Need I say more? ∎

Consultants

How to build an exceptional brand?

A brand that stands out boldly on store shelves, a brand that attracts customers and sales, a brand that builds your business and elevates your stature in the marketplace? Not easy. And when I bought The Republic of Tea, I had no expertise in this realm. None. But, lucky me, I found a true expert in the field: Al Ries. And Al worked wonders for us.

I first came across Al Ries through his business books. In 1981, he and Jack Trout, his partner in an acclaimed advertising agency, wrote a book that quickly became a classic in the world of marketing: *Positioning: The Battle for Your Mind*. The book bowled me over. Their governing idea was this: in the highly competitive world of business, companies need to go beyond PR, beyond clever advertising. As Al and Jack explained, companies need to position their products in a truly unforgettable way. As they put it, "Find an open hole in the mind, and become the first brand to fill it."

Their examples were compelling. Volvo took the word "safety" and made it synonymous with its brand. Fedex did the same with the word "overnight." Al and Jack praised 7UP for branding itself "the uncola," and they applauded the rental car agency Avis, the perennial runner-up to Hertz, for its distinctive and unforgettable message: "We try harder." Pure gold!

Al and Jack Trout wrote other illuminating books on marketing and advertising, and I loved every one of them. As Al expanded his influence, he soon had an eager protégé: his daughter Laura. As Laura later explained in an interview, she grew up watching television with her dad, listening to him critique the TV commercials. "The commercials were more important than 'M*A*S*H,'" she confided. "I always loved going to the agency when I was a kid. I pretended I worked there and made my own little ads."

The more I read by and about Al Ries, the more determined I became to meet the man. And Al was in the front of my mind when I bought The Republic of Tea. My investment was substantial, and I was totally new to the world of tea. Could Al help us blaze a winning path, a Road to Greatness? At that stage, I had never worked with a consultant before, and I had no idea how the process might work. And one question kept holding me back: what would a celebrated consultant like Al Ries charge for his services? I had no idea. By then Al and Jack Trout had parted ways, and Al and his daughter Laura had set up their own consulting firm, Ries & Ries, based in Atlanta, Georgia. They were far away from me and my team. What help might they be able to offer us? And at what price?

Despite my hesitations, one day I picked up the phone and called Al Ries. We had a brief, cordial chat and then I cut right to it: "So, Al, what do you charge?" Well, Al's answer floored me: his fee, he said, was $25,000 per day! Plus expenses! Shocked, I hung up and thought, well, that's that. At that stage, Al's fee was far beyond our means—and it was for services that remained a total mystery to me. Still, I was definitely intrigued: what would we get for our $25,000 a day? And what would be our return on that size of investment? I had no idea. So for guidance, I turned to Michael Patterson, a skilled CPA and the owner of the firm of Holt & Patterson, in Chesterfield, Missouri. I shared my hesitations with Mike, and he came right back with a salient question: "At that rate, Ron, how often would you use him?"

"Probably once every other year," I replied. With that, Mike offered me a workable solution: use Al Ries once every two years and put him on our books for $12,500 a year—a sum that we could definitely afford. I agreed and, as they say, the rest is history.

From there, Al flew out from Atlanta to see us in Southern Illinois and we spent eight amazing hours together. And I'll tell you this: we got our money's worth... and more! On the spot, Al shared with us his special gifts for branding and product presentation. We were beyond impressed, and later he helped us again when we launched our River Road Family Vineyards and Winery. In the process, Al and I built a friendship that lasted 20 years, right up to his death in 2022. And his daughter Laura became a trusted advisor for us as well. Now let me show you what Al and Laura taught us...

Taglines. When I started working with Al, I had no real understanding of what a good tagline could do. But as Al showed us, a winning tagline can do wonders for your image and your stature in the marketplace. Take Nike, for instance. Everybody knows its iconic tagline: "Just Do It." Yes! Those three words are instantly recognizable and unforgettable. It's a tagline that seals and elevates the Nike brand. With The Republic of Tea, we had a good reputation, but how could we distinguish ourselves from the big tea brands like Lipton, Twinings, and all the rest? Al's tagline nailed it:

"The Republic of Tea, Leading Purveyor of Premium Teas."

Spot on! And for our new winery? There are more than 540 wineries in Napa Valley, another 460 in Sonoma County, and thousands and thousands of wineries across America, France, Italy, Spain, Australia and beyond. Up against that kind of competition, how in the heck can you stand out to the millions and millions of consumers searching the wine aisles for a bottle to buy? Al's guidance: Think big. Think beyond country. Beyond wine-growing region. And think way beyond the usual wine-buying public. And the tagline we finally chose? "A Beautiful Experience." Yes! Who could ask for more?

Visual Hammers. What is a visual hammer? When we started working with Al and Laura, I had no clue. But as they taught us, visual hammers are powerful, distinctive design elements that help your products jump to the eye in fast, unforgettable ways. Every label of Duckhorn wine, for instance, features, front and center, an elegantly designed duck. Likewise, the labels of most Robert Mondavi Wines feature the winery's iconic archway and tower. For The Republic of Tea, Al and Laura led us to this: a small, artful teapot, a perfect symbol of exactly who we are.

Today I often sit back and shake my head in wonder. Forty years ago, I had no idea what a top consultant could do for your company, and the very idea of paying someone $25,000 for a single day's work seemed absolutely insane. But thanks to Al and Laura, I learned another golden lesson: to build your business, hire the best, most creative minds you can find—then listen and learn as they teach and guide you on your way. In our case, the truth is plain to see: without Al and Laura's wisdom and inspiration, our companies would not be the strong successes they are today. Listen and Learn—that simple philosophy will bring you magnificent rewards! I guarantee it!! ∎

The Message Map

As our learning deepened, and as we developed our expertise with Strategic Planning, PR, Branding, Taglines and Visual Hammers, the more I came to appreciate the importance of clear, effective communication. And then I had the good fortune to meet a man named Tripp Frohlichstein.

Tripp and I met in St. Louis in 1990, and he quickly became a family friend and my cherished guide into the high art of Effective Communication. As I built The Republic of Tea, Tripp helped me structure my presentations and he taught our staff how best to promote our products and our guiding values and spirit. As Tripp showed us, the best promotional messages have a strong emotional appeal, one that "hooks" the reader or the listener in an immediate, powerful way. And Tripp believed the best messages set that hook in seven seconds or less. Seven! And how to do that? Well, Tripp introduced us to an amazing tool that he had co-invented: The Message Map.

The Message Map is a visual representation of what Tripp calls your "Home Base." It puts your company in the center of the map, with all of its assets tightly defined, and then it shows the key benefits that radiate out from your Home Base. Here is the basic structure of Tripp's Message Map:

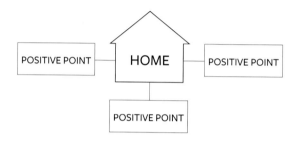

"The ideal Home Base appeals to virtually all audiences – customers, employees, and investors," Tripp explains. "It's important to have a Home Base, because your Home Base makes it easier for people to grasp what you are all about, as well as remember you. Your Home Base tells your audience exactly what you are about and *what's in it for them.*"

"What's in it for them." Yes, that's key. Many companies have messaging that basically says, "Aren't we great?" But as Tripp taught us, the most effective messaging highlights what your company does for others—and specifically for YOU! "We all make decisions based on emotions," Tripp explains. "A good Home Base will stir those emotions, and that will help you forge a stronger bond between you and your audience." For me, Tripp's message came down to this: Touching hearts is key to building your dreams.

Over and over I saw the importance of our Message Map. At The Republic of Tea we had it printed out for our team to use with our customers, and whenever I had to make a public presentation, I would have our Message Map at my fingertips and often projected onto a screen beside me. Later, at River Road Winery, we created another

Message Map, to help our employees clearly present our company, our products, and what makes us so special.

Thanks to Tripp, we learned so much about how to present our companies, and then he brought me another golden lesson, and he did so in a way that I will never forget. One day I was set to give an important speech at Culver Academies, my high school alma mater and the home of my school for entrepreneurship. I was a bit nervous about it, so I asked Tripp for some hands-on guidance. At his urging, I organized a full-scale dress rehearsal, for Tripp to watch and critique. But when Tripp arrived, he was not alone; he had with him his 14-year-old son Richie. What was this? Well, I delivered my speech, trying my best to make it lively and appealing, and afterwards Tripp said, "Okay, Ron, I'm not going to critique it. I'm going to leave that to Richie. He is, after all, the same age as your target audience."

With that, Richie cleared his throat and cut right to it: "Ditch the suit! Ditch the tie! The kids will find those way too stiff!" Okay! Done! And thanks to Richie, for the actual event I dressed very casually and that did help me develop an easy rapport with the Culver students. They loved the speech! And thanks to Tripp and Richie, I had learned an essential lesson for myself and for all public speakers: "Know your audience!"

Today I am so grateful for everything that Tripp Frohlichstein taught us: how to do winning presentations, how to create Message Maps, how to work with the media, and so much more. But the core issue here is always the same: Effective Communication. So my advice to you is this: find great advisors like Tripp. Create your own Message Maps. Teach your people how to become skilled communicators. Then sit back and enjoy the applause! ▪

Forum Moderator

In 1989, when my dad passed away, I took charge of our beverage distribution company, and while I was prepared for the challenge, and I had Uncle Julian right there to help me, the added responsibilities still weighed heavily on my mind and shoulders. The stress was constant and so were the challenges. But where to turn now for fresh wisdom and guidance?

Fortunately, one day a trusted friend of mine in Mt. Vernon saw that I was struggling a bit and he said to me, "Ron, have you ever heard of a group called YPO? The Young Presidents' Organization?" I had not heard of YPO, but right away I did some research and then I put in my application. To my delight, I was accepted into the Illini chapter of YPO and that became a crucial next step in my growth as a business and community leader.

At YPO, we had a member benefit called the "Forum Group." These were small groups of young presidents, only eight to ten per group, and we'd meet once a month to share our problems and concerns, seek advice, make connections, or maybe just sit around and chat in a warm, supportive way. Just what I needed! And the folks in our Forum Groups were remarkably diverse. We had truckers, farmers, bankers, people in the food business and more. But we were all presidents of our companies, and we were all dealing with the same kind of issues: How to run our companies. How to handle the ups and downs in our profits, and how to manage our teams and keep them happy and productive. Key issues for any business leader.

And every Forum Group had what was called a "Forum Moderator." This was one Young President who served as leader of the group and whose job was to set agendas, manage our meetings, and keep them focused and constructive. A big job! And to become a Forum Moderator, you didn't just raise your hand and volunteer. Oh, no. You had to *earn* the honor. And that meant going through a week-long training program in several essential leadership skills—namely those you need to manage eight or ten tough, hard-charging company presidents, all of them used to telling their staffs exactly what to do   and exactly how to do it. Not easy skills to master!

Still, I was up for the experience, and one day I volunteered for the Forum Moderator training program. Happily, I was accepted, and what superb training it proved to be! My week-long program was held in Dallas, and we had top-quality advisors, a handbook to follow, daily lessons, and practice sessions to polish our skills. This was not Leadership 101. This was Leadership 901. And it was exactly what I needed to run a Forum Group—and to better run our family business too. In the end, I passed the test and earned the honor of serving as a YPO Forum Moderator.

Today, as I look back, I see my training and my many years in YPO as an essential stepping stone to everything I went on to accomplish, not just in our company business, but also in the realms of Education, Sustainable Agriculture, Environmental Protection, and Corporate Social Responsibility. Thank you, YPO! Your training and your faith in me helped build my confidence, expand my horizons, and heighten my sense of purpose. And I am happy to report that my son Todd has become a prominent figure in the YPO as well. So for every young entrepreneur or business leader today, my advice for you is clear: look into the Young Presidents' Organization. It's a wonderful way to develop as a leader and to find friends and colleagues who will challenge you to keep learning, keep striving, and keep becoming the very best you can be. As I'm fond of saying, who could ask for more? ▪

14

Three Keys To Success

Lucky me! Thanks to YPO and to advisors like Barbara Shomaker, Al and Laura Ries, and Tripp Frolichstein, I was learning so much about how to build a business and build it to last. And then along came Dr. Robert Lefton, to put a golden crown on everything I was learning.

Bob Lefton was flat-out brilliant—and very generous with his wisdom. At Washington University in St. Louis, Bob did it all: a B.A. in Business and Psychology, an M.A. in Psychology, and then a Ph.D. in Psychology—all of this ideal training for what became his life's work: helping top executives of Fortune 500 companies master the arts of leadership, management, and staff development. In sum, how to build a company into the best it can be.

I first met Bob in the early 1990s, when I was building The Republic of Tea, and he became one of my most trusted friends and mentors. At the time, he was Chairman and CEO of Psychological Associates, a business consulting firm that was considered among the very best in the business, and every hour I spent with Bob I learned something new and important.

One day, for instance, I was chatting with Bob, about some of the issues I was dealing with at The Republic of Tea, and Bob leaned back and said, "Listen, Ron, business is really very simple: there are just three keys to success." I was stunned. "What? Just three? Will you share them with me?" Bob did share them and what an enlightening moment this became...

The First Key: Customer Satisfaction. As Bob explained, satisfying your customer is the first, essential key to business success. Whether you are creating a product, or providing a service, your first priority, always, always, is to provide everything your customer needs or wants. And more!

The Second Key: Employee Satisfaction. Take good care of your employees. Make sure they are satisfied with their pay, their benefits, their working conditions, the vision and attitude of their leaders, and, of course, the camaraderie and cooperation they enjoy with their fellow employees.

The Third Key: Cash Flow. Oh, my! For me, this was the big surprise. As Bob helped me understand, far too many entrepreneurs, and far too many business leaders fail to grasp the importance of Cash Flow. And they don't have at hand the one tool they need most: a weekly Cash Flow Statement, showing, in clear black and white, the health of their Cash Flow.

And the result? Many company leaders and their teams work their tails off to get their products into a Target, a Costco, or a local shop, and they pay—much of the money up front—all the costs of manufacturing and shipping the requested inventory. Then comes the wait. The wait for a Target, a Costco or some local business to pay their bill and place new orders—and keep the necessary cash flowing in. And if those company leaders are not properly monitoring their Cash Flow, and those expected funds don't arrive as expected, what happens? Cash Flow misery! Or even worse!

With his Three Keys to Success, Bob Lefton brought total clarity to my business needs. Today at The Republic of Tea and our River Road Family Vineyards and Winery, I know that if we satisfy our customers, if we satisfy our employees, and if we have a healthy Cash Flow—and every Wednesday I now have a Cash Flow Statement in hand— if we do all three of those things, and do them well, I'm confident. I know we're on course. We're moving steadily along our own Road to Greatness. Bless you, Bob Lefton!

Thanks to Bob and my other mentors, I now had a set of tools to help us build success: Strategic Plans. Taglines. Visual Hammers. Message Maps. Cash Flow Statements. And even a reliable measuring stick: Bob's Three Keys to Success. Exciting! And guess what? The best was still to come... ∎

15

Advisory Boards

In 1995, one year after I bought The Republic of Tea, Pam and I were feeling in need of a change. Life in our small country town in Southern Illinois was good, but we wanted a more stimulating, big city environment. So we up and moved to St. Louis. It was a good move, but then I often felt an aching void: The Republic of Tea was still in its formative stages, but now I had no YPO Forum Group to turn to for guidance and support. What to do?

Well, I thought about it for a long time and then it hit me: I'd create my own Forum Group! My own Advisory Board! I had no clue how to do it, so I turned to someone who did know: Dr. Robert Lefton. And again Bob was terrific. He agreed to serve on the board himself, and he gave me a list of top-quality executives he thought could be valuable members of my new Advisory Board. I then took each executive to lunch, to get to know them and to see if there was good chemistry between us. Well, everything clicked, and soon I had my own Advisory Board, a brain trust beautifully equipped to help put The Republic of Tea on a stronger and more lasting foundation.

Our board was remarkably talented and diverse. To complement Bob Lefton and his experience with Fortune 500 companies, we had one board member who specialized in helping small family businesses and managing acquisitions. Another was an expert in manufacturing—ideal for helping us produce our line of premium teas. Another member was a talented CPA and financial planner. Thanks to their different specialties and experience, I now had a team of top consultants, each on a retainer, and each able to guide me on specific aspects of building The Republic of Tea. Indeed, as it turned out, this was one of the smartest business moves I ever made.

Naturally, then, when I launched our River Road Family Vineyards and Winery, I decided to create another Advisory Board to help guide us on our way. And believe me, I needed all the help I could get! By then, the arts and sciences of viticulture and wine-making had evolved dramatically from the year I had spent at U.C. Davis, and I knew very little, too, about the inner workings of the wine industry. So I sought out industry experts who could help us build our new winery into a powerful, far-sighted force. Now, though, instead of calling it an Advisory Board, I gave the board a name more in tune with the California spirit: I called them my "Dream Team," and what a dream my Advisory Board proved to be! And they have provided wonderful support for our teams of vineyard specialists and winemakers too. Here's a little taste:

Diane DiRoma is the vice president and general manager of River Road Family Vineyards and Winery, and she has been my right hand for nearly two decades. Diane started out as our regional sales manager at The Republic of Tea, and she joined our River Road Vineyard team soon after we launched it. Ever since, Diane has overseen our wine-making operations and all of our strategic marketing and sales efforts. Diane also anchored our campaign to earn our standing as a Certified B Corporation. Pure gold!

Along the way, Diane earned her MBA from the School of Business and Economics at Sonoma State University and she also serves on the board of directors of the Russian River Valley Winegrowers. In sum, Diane is indispensable!

Ed Morris is our chief winemaker, and he brings to us a unique background of art and craftsmanship. Ed's great-grandfather built violins. His grandfather was a clock maker. His father was a carpenter. Ed grew up in Sonoma County's Russian River Valley, and through a summer job he learned how to craft the oak barrels that are so crucial to the art of wine-making. Ed apprenticed with some of the master French coopers who had come to work in California, and soon he was crafting barrels for local wine-makers. He then studied wine-making at Santa Rosa Junior College and then at U.C. Davis. With his wealth of expertise, in 2010 we hired Ed for our team, and in 2020 we made him our chief winemaker. And what a great job he has done for us!

Mark Greenspan, another of our key advisors, is a leading expert in sustainability, specifically regarding micro-climates, irrigation practices, vineyard nutrition, crop loads, grape maturation, and weather and climate influences too. With his expertise and hands-on guidance, Mark helps teach our viticulture and wine-making teams and make them the best in their fields.

Dr. Lee Katz also brings an exceptional background to our Dream Team. Lee grew up in Flossmoor, Illinois, southwest of Chicago. A brilliant student, he entered the University of Illinois at the ripe old age of 16, and he later graduated in the top three percent of his class. From there, Lee studied medicine at the University of Chicago Medical School and he did a residency at Yale University. In 1986, Yale invited Lee to join their faculty.

Later, still hungry for more, Lee went to business school and earned his MBA. With his unique blends of expertise, I couldn't resist: I invited Lee Katz to join us at The Republic of Tea and serve as our "Minister of Health." Later he joined our River

Road Winery, to help our staff and our customers understand the health benefits of following a diet of good food and good wine, in moderation of course. Lee Katz has been worth his weight in gold!

The same is true of Dr. Elizabeth Thach. Liz is amazing. She earned her B.A. in English from Notre Dame de Namur, in Belmont, California. Then she earned her M.A. in Organizational Communication and Management at Texas Tech, then a Ph.D. in Human Resource Development from Texas A&M. From there Liz became an advisor to several Fortune 500 companies. Then Liz fell in love with fine wine. And what did she do? To develop her expertise and her palate, Liz went on a tasting tour of many of the finest wine-growing regions in the world. From there, she studied viticulture and enology and earned the coveted title of Master of Wine. Before long, Liz was named Distinguished Professor of Wine and Management at Sonoma State University. I met Liz at Sonoma State, and I simply could not resist: I invited Liz Thach to join our Dream Team. A terrific move!

So, dear readers, my advice to you is simple: Be Bold! Think Big! Create your own Advisory Boards! Your own Dream Teams! Find the most gifted and experienced people you can find, and then convince them to come join your team and share their wisdom. You'll never regret it! Still, building dreams is never easy. And if, as you go, you ever need a smile or a fresh jolt of energy, you might frame this quote and keep it right on your desk:

"Creativity is intelligence having fun!"—Albert Einstein ■

Feng Shui

Wisdom. Guidance. Inspiration. Listen and Learn. In this hallowed light, I need to tell you now about a man named Roy Fong.

Roy Fong holds a special place in the history of premium tea in America—and a special place in my personal history as well. Roy was born and raised in Hong Kong, China, and as early as the age of six Roy developed a love of Chinese teas. On his way to or from school, he would linger at food stands, smelling the teas being prepared, and when people would offer him a cup, Roy would eagerly savor the different aromas and tastes. He was enthralled! Out walking in the streets, if he caught a scent, Roy would follow it straight into a tea shop, to taste and learn and enjoy a cup. And that was just the beginning...

When Roy was 13, his family emigrated to the United States, and when he turned 21, Roy made his first trip back to China. There he went from tea shop to tea shop, tasting, learning, and asking questions. And right there his life-long passion was born. Soon Roy Fong set up a business importing and selling Chinese teas to restaurants in America—and a major part of his work was education. Many American consumers and restaurant owners knew next to nothing about premium Chinese teas—and they knew even less about the special arts and culture that produce the finest Chinese teas. Then, in 1993, Roy made an audacious leap: he and his wife Grace opened the first Imperial Tea Court, in San Francisco's Chinatown. Along with a rich selection of teas, Roy and Grace soon began offering dim sum delicacies, and their business took off! Then they opened a second Imperial Tea Court in Berkeley.

Naturally, this was a man I had to meet!

I met Roy soon after I bought The Republic of Tea and we became fast friends. And this was key: in 1995 Roy took me on my first trip to China, to meet the finest tea producers and to understand the special culture that produces the finest teas. This was more than a fabulous education; it was a life-changing experience. The majority of the world's finest teas come from four countries: China, Japan, India, and Sri Lanka, but with Roy as my guide, my education began in China and I could not have asked for more.

During my travels with Roy, we met with many tea growers and suppliers, and our hosts would tell us about the leaves they grew, how the leaves are nourished and harvested, and always, always, our hosts would then lead us out into their tea gardens, to taste their teas and help us appreciate the spirit that goes into their crafting. And wherever we went, I kept hearing the words "Feng Shui"—Wind and Water—and Roy explained that those two words represent a wisdom and culture going back 5,000 years or more.

As I learned, Feng Shui is a philosophy and a set of guidelines designed to foster an environment of balance and harmony, with calming spaces that encourage people to pause, to reflect, and to more fully appreciate the world around them. As I came to understand, Feng Shui is all about placement, about movement, about the harmonious flow of light and energy. And in China I found myself marveling at how the walkways curved like a flowing river, how the work spaces had tables and chairs opening direct to the light, and how ponds or bubbling fountains are often used to enhance the flow of energy. All this was totally new for a guy from Southern Illinois, and I simply fell in love with the wisdom and spirit of Feng Shui. Thank you, Roy Fong!

Then, of course, I had to deepen my learning. I read several books about Feng Shui, I talked with experts, and right away I realized that we had to weave Feng Shui thinking and principles into my dreams for The Republic of Tea. And not just into our buildings and surroundings, but also into our wider approach to life and business. Placement, movement, energy flow. Yes! When we began designing a new production facility for The Republic of Tea, in Nashville, Illinois, I was fortunate enough to find Lenore Weiss, a gifted architect in Chicago who was an expert in the teachings of Feng Shui.

Lenore came to our site in Nashville, she understood the many layers of what we wanted to achieve, and she wove Feng Shui principles into the heart and soul of our project. From our entryway, to our hallways, to our offices, and right down to the placement of our tables and chairs—everything felt natural and free. Everything just felt right. My wife Pam and I were delighted and so impressed that we then wove Feng Shui principles into our new home in St. Louis, and we did it again later when we opened a new office for The Republic of Tea in Larkspur, California. And we all loved the results!

Naturally, when we designed our new River Road Family Vineyards and Winery, I was insistent that we weave Feng Shui principles and spirit into our planning. And I soon found another gifted expert to guide our way: Barbara Lyons Stewart. Barbara was terrific and the results were just as I had hoped. From the curving pathway into our winery, to our smooth, rounded walls and work spaces, to our tasting area, one flight up and looking out across an unspoiled expanse of vineyard—a space often dancing with brilliant sunlight and color—everything feels calm, relaxed, and in harmony with Nature. And in our lab, where our winemaker pursues his craft and works his magic, a gentle light flows in and brightens his workspace. Who could ask for more? A touch of ancient Chinese wisdom in the heart of California Wine Country. ▪

PART FOUR

HONOR AND SHARE

Great things in business are never done by one person. They're done by a team of people.

■ STEVE JOBS ■

Exercise

In the early years, when I was working with my dad and learning the business, I was a very busy guy. There was constant work. And constant stress. I was doing everything I could to succeed and prove my worth. And right there I realized that getting regular exercise was essential to my daily routine. It gave me time to relax, clear my head, and make better decisions.

So I set out to establish for myself a daily exercise routine. By then, James F. Fixx's book, *The Complete Book of Running,* first published back in 1977, was already a classic in the field of health and exercise, and I used it to develop a daily program to reduce stress, heighten my energy, keep my body moving and my thinking clear. And the program worked. I felt great!

So great, in fact, that I wanted to share the benefits with the rest of our team. So I started encouraging everyone on our team to start getting regular exercise. My approach was very informal. I didn't push weight training, yoga, Pilates or aerobic exercise. No, I was just urging everyone to take a little time off to exercise, even if it was only for some stretching or a walk outside in the fresh air. Still, I was serious about it, and going forward we decided to include a section on exercise and health in our company handbook.

Later, when I bought The Republic of Tea, I expanded the effort, with a special feature: every year we gave our team quality workout shoes from New Balance. We had New Balance specialists come in, measure everyone's feet to get just the right fit, with the right soles and support, all this to encourage them to go out and get some exercise. To that same end, we gave each of our employees a yearly $500 grant to use for a gym membership or a fitness center fee. The costs were not significant, but our guiding message was:

We care about you! We care about your health and well-being! We're building a team, we want it to be a happy, highly motivated team, and we want you to be a devoted member of our team... for a long time to come! ■

18

Profit Sharing

When it comes to team building, again I have to tip my hat to my dad.

Like all the best business leaders, Dad kept his eye on the big picture, on building a company that would be solid and long-lasting, with a stellar reputation at home and throughout the business community. And for Dad, building a solid, long-lasting company depended on… People! On hiring the right people, for the right jobs, and keep our team happy, motivated, and loyal to our cause. But how do you build a winning team, one with that kind of commitment and spirit? For my dad, this was the key: Honor and Share.

Let me give you an example. Back in 1972, when I first joined the company, Dad decided to create something new: a profit-sharing plan for all of our employees, a plan that would honor their service and keep our people loyal and motivated, hopefully for their entire working lives. As usual, Dad started the process by getting the best advice he could find. In this case, he went to the trust department of a high-quality bank, and with them he evaluated many different profit-sharing formulas, including plans where employees contribute part of their own earnings to a company-wide profit-sharing plan. But that formula was not for Dad. Oh, no. He believed that if our company had a good year, all contributions to our retirement plan should come from company earnings—not from contributions from our staff. Dad's guiding ethos was clear: we're all in this together; if we all work hard and we work well, everyone wins—and everyone should profit too!

Dad's formula worked beautifully, as I saw first-hand over the next two decades. Naturally, when I took over The Republic of Tea, I brought in the same profit-sharing model. Later, at our River Road Family Vineyards and Winery, I continued the tradition. Profit-sharing plans are now a permanent part of our DNA, and our plans have improved over the years. Today, for instance, our employees can determine how they want their funds invested, and they have access to their accounts 24/7, via their computer or cell phone. Also, there's a new law, the Safe Harbor Act, that calls for a minimum contribution of 3 percent of gross wages to our kind of plan. The result? Thanks to my dad's foresight, and our honoring his tradition, many of our employees stay with us throughout their entire careers! And when they do retire, they do so with a very nice nest egg. It won't cover all their needs, of course, but it certainly helps. And let me add an important point here...

We live in turbulent times. And we have all seen the headlines: this corporate giant or that is laying off 5,000 workers or more. And behind those headlines is the pain we rarely see: those employees and their families are abruptly sent out into the cold. And how are they notified? Too often with a terse email or a perfunctory thank you. Brutal. But that's not us. If I have to let a single employee go, I agonize over the decision, and I often lose sleep over it too. I simply cannot imagine having to lay off thousands of people at a single clip. That's not for me. Like my dad, I prefer to think of our staff as our extended family, and I do my best to honor them as such. That's us: Honor and Share. And the rewards have been beautiful. My wonderful executive assistant, Libby Griffin, has been with me for 45 years! Imagine that!

Almost every year, our practice of Honor and Share brings me another lovely dividend. At year's end, when our employees get their profit-sharing statements, they often send me grateful thank you notes. I love those notes and I save all of them, in part as a reminder of my father's wisdom. A recent note I received made my heart sing: "Dear Ron... Just a note to thank you for the generous profit-sharing this year. Though the past couple of years have presented financial challenges in the world over all, it's comforting to know that The Republic of Tea is going strong. Here's to 2023!"

Here's to you, Dad. You had the right spirit! Honor and Share! And I will be forever grateful for everything you taught us! ■

19

The Caliper Profile

How to build a winning team?

A team with the right people in the right jobs, jobs where you and your people feel it's the right fit, a job where they will feel confident they have what it takes to succeed and prosper? Putting the right people in the right jobs is always a stiff challenge, but right here I will show you how we learned to handle it, thanks to an amazing tool called The Caliper Profile.

The Caliper Profile is an objective, science-based assessment of a job candidate's personality traits, their various strengths and weaknesses, and the specific jobs where they are most likely to succeed. The Caliper Profile is based on nearly six decades of research, and it evaluates people based on 22 different character traits, giving employers a clear picture of a candidate's likely short- and long-term performance in this job or that. Over the years, I have interviewed scores of candidates for a specific post, and their Caliper Profiles have helped me evaluate those candidates in a way that extends far beyond what I was able to learn in a traditional hiring interview. And over and over, the Caliper Profiles have helped me make the right decision.

Let me show you how the Caliper process works. Back when I was working in my dad's liquor distribution company we decided to expand our reach across a broader geographic area. We became a Gallo wine distributor at the time, and we had to hire eight new sales reps in one fell swoop. Not easy! And we had a lot on the line. So I started doing interviews and right away I found the process terribly confusing. For eight positions, I had some 50 applicants! Which one to choose? And I was hiring, too, for positions in different locations, with different costs of living. As I say, it was not easy...

But The Caliper Profile came to my rescue. Their evaluations were developed by a company called Caliper, now called Talogy, headquartered in Princeton, New Jersey. In this case, I saw no need to test all 50 of our applicants. Instead, for one key sales job I narrowed the field down to two very promising candidates, and then I ordered Caliper tests and profiles for each of them. The results were enlightening. The Caliper tests are scored on a scale of zero to 100, and one of our candidates scored a 90, and the other scored a 60. This was telling: according to the Caliper test score, it meant that the candidate who scored only 60 had a 40 percent chance of failing in our position. Not good odds! That was helpful to know, but the wider Caliper Profile then provided us with additional layers of information.

For instance, Caliper assesses what it calls "abstract reasoning," a primary element of human intelligence. Again, that's helpful. But Caliper also has a category that assesses a candidate's likely ability to succeed in the sales arena. That category is called "Ego Drive." In any industry, sales are tough: you make the call, you make your pitch, and you do your best to close the deal—and maybe earn a commission in the process. But here's the raw truth: whether you're selling cars, or paint, or, for this job, cases and cases of Gallo wines—what sales people face, every single day, even every hour, is this: Rejection. Failure. Constant no's. But Ego Drive evaluates a person's resilience, his or her capacity to get smacked down, time after time, but then to jump right back up and charge into battle. And that requires Ego Drive.

Well, thanks largely to what I learned through the Caliper process, I hired eight young men for our expanded sales team, and they proved to be fabulous: hard-driving salesmen with ferocious ego drives. On Fridays we would have our weekly sales meeting, and our sales guys would come in with a swagger and really go at it. One would brag about his sales numbers for the week, then another would retort, "Shoot, man, that's nothing! Look how I did this week!" On and on our guys would go, in high spirits, the eight all trying to outdo each other. It was great fun—and it also produced terrific results: month after month our sales volume soared!

The Caliper Profiles were useful in a variety of other ways. My own Caliper Profile showed that I don't have a strong ego drive. Okay. But I then used that result to my advantage. If, back in the early days, I was at The Fancy Food Show, and I wanted to close a big new deal there, I made sure that our national sales manager was right there beside me, to clinch the deal. And I knew that she was far better at that than I am! Thank you, Caliper!

Right here, let me quote from my own Caliper Profile, to give you a feel for the way Caliper evaluates candidates and what roles they are best suited for: "Ron's ego drive is relatively mild. He simply does not derive a great deal of ego gratification from the conquest of another individual. This does not mean he cannot sell; it simply means that the overall management function is more important to him than the sales conquest." Yup! Spot-on! I am far better at managing than I am with sales!

The Caliper Profiles have also helped us understand what kinds of people to hire for our positions in customer service and client management. For those jobs, Caliper recommends hiring candidates who score high in this category: "Empathy." Yes indeed! In line with this Caliper category, our best hires have usually been women, and they have been superb. When they are on the phone, dealing with an angry client, for instance, they have just the right touch: "Oh, we're soooo sorry this happened! But don't worry! You're such a valued customer, we will fix it right away!" That, folks, is Empathy in action. And again, thank you Caliper!

Over the years, The Caliper Profiles have been for us a wondrous tool. That said, I never crow too loudly about Caliper—I don't want to tip off our competitors!—but thanks to their research and profiles I now have a much deeper understanding of how to hire the right people, for the right jobs, and then how to help them grow, succeed and prosper—for the greater good of all of us! And that, for sure, is a lesson worth its weight in gold! ▪

The Sibson Way

Hiring the right people, for the right job, is an essential step in building a winning team. And thank you, Caliper. But now comes a stiffer challenge: keeping your people happy, motivated, and devoted, long-term, to your company. Here money is key: making sure your employees have salaries and compensation packages that honor their performance and do so in line with industry standards. But how to do that in a dependable way?

In the early days of building The Republic of Tea, at our base in Southern Illinois, we would have annual reviews of our employees' pay and other benefits, to be sure their compensation packages were satisfying for our team and in line with the norms of our industry. In those early days, the process was fairly straightforward. But as we expanded, things got a little tricky. Suddenly I had sales people living and working for us across the United States. We had an office in San Francisco, and I had marketing and PR people I never had before. There were other issues too. The cost of living in California, for instance, was far higher than it was in St. Louis, or at our headquarters in Southern Illinois. How best to handle all of that?

Thanks to a member of our Advisory Board, I found the answer: a compensation specialty group called Sibson Consulting. They are now called Segal Consulting, and they have offices all around the country. And these folks are fantastic. They help companies, big and small, make sure that their compensation packages for a given position, in a given locale, are proper and satisfying for both the company and their staffer. They also give guidance on matters such as cost-of-living adjustments, the typical size of bonuses within a given industry, and more—all based on sophisticated research they conduct across the United States. And as soon as I started working with Sibson, I could feel a huge weight lift from my shoulders.

With Sibson consultants guiding us, we set up a comprehensive review process for all of our top executives. The review, which we update every two years, is based on their time and position with us, and it sets forth their base pay, their bonus potential, and it takes into account any changes in the executive's responsibilities within our company. Our aim is simple: to make sure our team members are happy and well-satisfied with the way their careers and their pay packages are advancing.

As part of the process, I would meet with each executive and show them the Sibson data for our industry, so they could see, right there in black and white, how they compared with others in equivalent positions. In these sessions, my message to them was always clear and reassuring: We value your work. We honor your commitment to us. And, in response, we are determined to be caring, consistent, and generous, so that you are totally happy working for us today and throughout the years to come. Our formula: Honor and Share, build great teams, and build them to last!

To my delight, our teams have embraced the Sibson process. With it, they can see that we are honest and caring company leaders and that we are committed to being reliable long-term partners for them and their families. And thanks to Sibson's research and resulting data, they can see that their compensation packages are fair and appropriate. Thanks to all this, many of our top people have remained loyal to us throughout their entire careers—a true blessing for all of us. So we thank you, Sibson/Segal! We have relied on your care and expertise for 17 years... and we're still counting! ▪

Heads Held High

Let me tell you now about *Trillion Dollar Coach*, a book written as an homage to a brilliant business and life coach named Bill Campbell.

Bill was quite a guy. During his many years as a football player and then as a coach, Bill Campbell mastered the difficult arts of leadership and team-building, and from his life in football he went on to become a trusted mentor for many Silicon Valley giants, including Larry Page and Sergei Brin, the co-founders of Google, Eric Schmidt a long-time CEO and chairman of Google, and many others, including some fella named Steve Jobs. Bill advised and inspired all of them, along with many others at Google, Apple, Amazon, Intuit and other pioneering companies. Later, Google's Eric Schmidt and others drew Bill's wisdom and teachings together in *Trillion Dollar Coach*.

I loved the book, and Bill Campbell brought me valuable insights into how to build our teams at The Republic of Tea and our River Road Family Vineyards and Winery.

And one passage, just a few pages long, really hit home for me: it was titled "Heads Held High," and it dealt with one of every business leader's most difficult and dreaded tasks: Firing people. Firing *your* people. People you hired. People who have put their lives and their futures in your hands, and often the futures of their families too.

I had fired people, and I knew those agonizing decisions all too well. And every time I had to do it, one question was always front and center in my mind: How do you break the news? How do you tell someone, "Sorry, but your career and your life here are over. Your dreams of success with us are finished." Today, big companies often lay off thousands of people at a time, and they often do it by email—with all the cold cruelty that conveys. That was not for me. Still, how do you deliver the heart-wrenching news?

Well, here is the golden lesson I learned from Bill Campbell via the *Trillion Dollar Coach*: when you have to let a staffer go, do it right, do it in person, and be sure to emphasize the many good things that he or she did for your company. Show your appreciation. Praise what they were able to achieve. And be specific in your praise. Then you can say, with truth and conviction, "We are so grateful, but going forward it's just not going to work out for us. Your future will be much brighter somewhere else." When you show your respect that way, you are handling a difficult situation with care and consideration, and you are honoring your employee's contributions and enabling them to leave with their "Head Held High." To show you the wisdom and heart in Bill's approach, let me share with you a little story...

At our winery, we once had a very bright individual who was just not working out for us. Her field was marketing, and she was very talented, but her skills and manner were just not a good fit for what we needed. We tried, but we finally came to the conclusion that for us—and for her—this was just not going to work. The task of delivering our decision fell to Diane DiRoma, the general manager of our winery. Diane and I discussed the situation, and I shared with her Bill Campbell's advice, and I know that Diane handled the situation with consummate care. Still, I figured our decision would be a very harsh blow for our staffer. But do you know what happened next?

Soon thereafter, Diane spotted the employee at a local restaurant, and the staffer excitedly waved Diane over. "Oh no," Diane thought. "What's this?" But to Diane's relief, the staffer was bursting with joy: "Diane, you did the best thing you could have done for me! As I see now, my position with you just wasn't right, for me or for you, and guess what? I have a fabulous new job now—and it's just what I needed! So thank you!"

Perfect! What a golden lesson: Heads Held High! And, in my eyes, that wisdom symbolizes the kind of leadership I admire, the kind that top-quality people crave and are eager to follow. Thank you, Bill Campbell! ∎

Weekend Work

When I started working with my dad, back in 1972, we worked seven days a week. Every week. That was our routine and I never questioned it.

On Saturday and Sunday mornings, we would start with a trip to the post office, then we'd go into our office to handle whatever needed to be done. Often on Saturdays and Sundays we'd work just a half day, but Dad felt it was important to maintain the routine and to lead by example, to show our staff our commitment, and I was happy to join him. Even when I married Pam, two years later, I kept to that routine. And even when we had our kids, and I found myself missing their soccer games and other Saturday activities, I still went with Dad into the office on weekends. I knew no other way.

Then I discovered someone new: Sam Walton. Sam was a true American pioneer, and at that time he was deemed the richest man in the world. And, of course, I had to read all about him. Sam had been born and raised on small family farms in Oklahoma and Missouri. Life on the farm was tough, and money was scarce for the Walton family, but young Sam was determined to learn and succeed and build a better life for his family.

Early on, Sam joined the Boy Scouts and soon became the youngest boy in Missouri to ever earn the rank of Eagle Scout. During the worst of The Great Depression, every morning, before school, Sam milked the family cow, bottled the milk, and delivered it to their neighbors. On the side, he also had a paper route and sold magazine subscriptions, to earn extra money. Later, Sam enrolled at the University of Missouri, where he studied hard, waited on table in exchange for free meals, and he immersed himself in the disciplines of economics and business. Upon graduating, at the top of his class, Sam Walton landed a job as a management trainee at a J.C. Penney store in Des Moines, Iowa—earning the princely sum of $75 a month!

In the early days of World War II, Sam joined the U.S. Army, first working in a munitions plant, then serving in the U.S. Army Intelligence Corps. After the war, and backed by a $20,000 loan from his father-in-law and $5,000 he had saved from his Army service, Sam Walton purchased a small Ben Franklin variety shop in Newport, Arkansas. As always, he was determined to learn and succeed, and from those humble beginnings Sam Walton went on to start two giant enterprises that would earn him a fortune and change the face of commercial life in America: Walmart and Sam's Club. What a guy, and what an inspiration he became for me!

In one early book about the man, *Sam Walton, The Inside Story of The World's Richest Man*, I found a section that seemed to be written expressly for me. The section was called "Weekend Work," and in it Sam Walton argued that no one should ever work seven days a week. Ever! Come on, he said, seven days out of seven, that's almost your entire life! Instead, he advocated that everyone work only five days out of every seven; five was enough, he said, and it was much healthier for your body, mind, and spirit. You can imagine my reaction. Here was hard-earned wisdom from the richest man in the world; who was I to argue?

I didn't want to interfere with my dad's lifelong routine, but after he passed away, I established a five-day work week for myself and our teams at The Republic of Tea and later at our River Road Family Vineyards and Winery. And right away I saw Sam Walton's wisdom in action: our company morale improved—and so did everyone's home life! Our team worked hard all week long, and they were now delighted to have their weekends free. Even at the winery, instead of opening on weekends, I hold to Sam Walton's advice. And our teams tell me they really appreciate our guiding philosophy and spirit: Work hard and share! We're all in this together! ∎

23

Women, They Rule

When I was growing up in Southern Illinois, the business world was dominated by men. And that was especially true in my father's domain, the wholesale wine and liquor business. At that time, there were almost no women in the liquor business. Companies big and small were run mostly by men, and there was a general belief that women didn't belong in the liquor business. And that was the way my dad operated too.

I wanted to change that. After my father passed away, I vowed to do things differently in our distribution company. Soon we had a regional position open for a sales person to call on restaurants, and we had a fine woman candidate named Shirley Watson. I knew that hiring a woman would create quite a stir in our company and in the industry, but I went ahead and hired Shirley anyway. And she was fantastic! She could sell! Our clients loved her! Shirley understood our products, how to make them appealing, and how to build warm, lasting relationships with all of our partners! And right there I made a fundamental shift in our hiring practices.

When we made the leap into the bottled water business, with Clearly Canadian, I hired women to help our regional sales people, and again those women did a marvelous job. They were quick learners, wonderful listeners, and they had just the right ability to connect with our customers and sell our products. And what an education they gave me! Naturally, then, when I bought The Republic of Tea, the first person I hired was a brilliant graphic designer named Gina Amador. Through Gina and others, I learned that the majority of people who were buying our teas were women, and Gina really opened my eyes, showing me how to use color and the design of our labels and packaging to appeal to those women shoppers. Thanks to Shirley Watson and Gina Amador, I learned a magnificent lesson: Women, They Rule!

From there, I became absolutely bullish about putting women into key leadership roles. And the results have been dazzling. Today, at The Republic of Tea production plant in Nashville, Illinois, our VP of Operations is Melissa Meador, and she very ably manages our staff of 147 people. Likewise, at our winery we are blessed to have Diane DiRoma as our general manager. With her MBA and her many years of experience, Diane keeps us all on our toes, and we have several women serving as our regional managers and they do a terrific job too. Today I can't say it loud enough: Women, They Rule! ∎

Manicure for Good Impression

In this same vein, let me share with you a fun little story…

When I was 14, just starting out at the Culver Military Academy—now called Culver Academies—in Indiana, I was a "plebe," meaning a brand new cadet, and as part of our training we had rigorous inspections.

We had inspections of our rooms, to see that our beds were properly made, that our floors were spotless, that our closets were orderly, and that our uniforms and physical appearance measured up to Culver's exacting standards. Part of that inspection was our hands and fingernails, and the rule here was iron-clad: your nails had to be properly cut—and there had better not be any dirt under those nails! None! We were officers in training, tomorrow's leaders in training, and Culver Military Academy expected us plebes to follow its standards to the letter.

From that training, I soon began a lifelong practice: having my nails professionally cut and polished. Throughout my college years, and my courtship and marriage with Pam, and then in my business career, I have enjoyed getting manicures on a regular basis. It just makes me feel good, to be presentable right down to the tips of my fingers. So today, when I talk to young entrepreneurs and business leaders, I often tout the virtues of manicures... and what's the reaction? Often laughter or even ridicule! A manicure? Good for business? Come on, Ron! Who are you kidding?

One day I gave a talk to our Young Presidents' Organization, and I asked them, "How many of you get manicures?" Out of about 38 people in the room, only two raised their hands. Well, I decided to have some fun with that. So I passed out $20 bills and urged all the young presidents to go get a manicure, on me, just to see how people reacted. Soon thereafter, I received a note from one young president telling me his wife was shocked by his decision—and shocked too by how attractive his hands looked!

Now let me put a little icing on the cake. When I started out in the wine business, with our River Road Family Vineyards and Winery, our most important customer was the retail group Total Wine & More, and it continues to be our most important customer today. They are a superb partner to have, and they often hold special wine tastings right in their stores. To learn as much as I could about how best to present and sell our wines, I decided to manage a few tastings at Total Wine & More, to see people's reactions as they tried our wines. Right away I saw that the majority of people who shop at Total Wine and enjoy these tastings are women, and let me tell you what I discovered, right there on day one...

As I presented our wines, I had several women gathered around me, watching as I lifted a bottle and filled their glasses, and what was the first thing many of the women noticed? My hands! And my nails! Instantly, I could see that the cleanliness of my hands and the polish of my nails put them at ease, and some of the women even said, "Wow,

Ron, who does your nails?" And did these women wind up buying our wines? You bet they did! And these tastings at Total Wine & More became a fabulous way for us to sell our wines and build our business. As I'm fond of saying, "Women, They Rule," and if you want to develop a strong, lasting bond with your women customers, go get your nails done! ■

Thank You Notes

Speaking of women who rule, right here I want to pay tribute to a very special woman, my wife Pam. By nature, Pam is thoughtful and considerate, and she introduced me to something that proved to be vitally important in building our teams and our stature in the business community: the power of a personal thank you note.

In today's world, in business and beyond, so much is handled by curt emails, or by text messages, or by a quick, shouted "Thank you!" between meetings. But as Pam helped me see, one of the most meaningful things you can do is sit down and write someone a warm, personal thank you note.

Today at The Republic of Tea and our River Road Family Vineyards and Winery we have lovely printed cards that we use to express our appreciation, to our staff, to our suppliers, or to our visitors. And we supply boxes of cards to our team, for them to write warm, personal thank you notes whenever they feel it's appropriate. Still, our team members often ask me, "Ron, what should I say in the thank you note?" One thing I always suggest is this: thank people for their time. The time they gave you. Time is precious. And we need to honor it when people give us their time and attention. I think a personal thank you note also conveys something deeper: the values we hold dear, for ourselves, for our families, and for the wider communities we are determined to serve.

Today I love sharing this lesson with business leaders and with the students in our entrepreneurship program at Culver Academies. And one year I got the sweetest dividend. After their first semester at Culver, I got about 30 hand-written thank you notes from our students. They shared with me the lessons they were learning, and how important those were for the lives and the careers they were eager to build. And I can tell you this: those thank you notes meant more to me than I can possibly express. Touching hearts, and helping young people build their dreams—who could ask for more? ∎

26

The Five P's

Over the years, as I strived to build our businesses, I developed a mindset, an innovative approach to planning and preparation that has served me and my teams well. I call it The Five P's. Let me show you how it works...

The Five P's are: Pre. Plan. Prevents. Poor. Performance. In sum, "Pre-Planning Prevents Poor Performance." Those Five P's can work wonders for you. Take, for instance, a basic business task: Travel Plans.

Given all of today's travel delays and disruptions, my teams and I always plan our travel with The Five P's in mind. A case in point: I recently had to go to Washington D.C. for an important meeting. It was an evening meeting, and I could have chosen to fly in from St. Louis that very same day. But no. Just to be on the safe side, I flew in the day before, and boy am I glad I did! A bit of bad weather kicked up the day of the meeting and most of the flights from St. Louis were cancelled! But thanks to the Five

P's, I walked into my meeting relaxed and prepared, and we carried the day. Hurrah! Now let me give you a more substantive example...

One year my executive team at The Republic of Tea and I were weighing a bold new move, and to evaluate the idea we decided to set up a meeting that would bring all the major players together—plus a few outside experts we hoped could help guide our way. The question at hand was clear: Could we turn this new idea into a shining success? What would it take? And what were the risks? With so much at stake, what did I do? Guided by the Five P's, I spent *months* preparing for that first critical meeting. Not weeks. Not one chaotic weekend, just before the meeting. Months! And as a first step, I learned all I could about the people who would be participating. Using Google, LinkedIn, and the archives of *The Wall Street Journal* and *The New York Times*, I was able to gain valuable information about each person, details we then used to personalize and refine our approach.

Our next step? Preparing strong presentation materials. We needed to present our company, of course, but we also needed to present our new idea, the challenges of the market we would be working in, and we needed to make clear the specific results we hoped to achieve—and how fast. At the heart of this was an essential lesson I had learned over the years: a strong, persuasive presentation sends a crucial message to your own team and also to your prospective partners—we're pros, and we're exemplary partners too; we will do whatever is necessary to satisfy *your goals*, as well as our own. And I am happy to report that all of our intensive planning paid off beautifully! So there it is: Pre-Planning Prevents Poor Performance.

There is a golden truth inside the Five P's: the most successful partnerships are not built on numbers or sales results. They are built with people, people who share common goals and values, people who want to build a better future together. And that's a lesson we all should treasure! ■

If You Are on Time, You're Late!

It started at age 14, when I went away to school, to the Culver Military Academy. The school has since dropped the "Military" from its name, but back then the routine and spirit were pure Army/Navy/Marine Corps: Rise and Shine! For me, the Culver routine was strict and demanding, and every day I felt challenged to the core. And each day started with a 6 a.m. ritual called "The Lineup." For The Lineup we had to arrive properly dressed, combed, our hands clean and our shoes polished. And for The Lineup there was one iron-clad rule: you cannot arrive late. Ever!

I have honored the discipline of the lineup throughout my life and my business career. And over the years I learned to take it a step further: if you are on time, I believe you are actually running a little late. As I saw over and over, for a meeting, a Zoom call, or a business lunch, it's essential to arrive on time—and it's even better to arrive 10 or 15 minutes early!

What are the benefits of arriving early? For one thing, arriving early lowers your blood pressure. No need to fret about being late, or arriving at a meeting rumpled or disorganized; arriving early helps you feel confident and composed, ready to present yourself in the best possible light. It also sends an important message to the other person, or the group of people you're meeting with: you honor their presence, you respect their time. And that helps you build a solid relationship based on confidence and trust.

Also, if you're attending a big, important conference, as we often do in the fine foods industry, I found that it always pays to arrive a little early. When we arrive, there is always a big table out front, with the name tags of everyone attending. By arriving early, we can look over the tags and decide who we want to be sure to meet. We can also grab seats up front, to be in the heart of the action and close to the people leading the conference. That's far better, of course, than being stuck in the back of the room!

What's my larger message here? Leadership. Be early. Be out in front. Set an example. Just by taking what I had learned at Culver, from the daily rigor and personal responsibility of the lineup, I was showing my staff the values I wanted my organization to embody. In any field, it is not easy to reach the top. But that was my goal, for myself and my teams, and being a little early was a small, but very effective step toward reaching that goal.

To my mind, Leadership carries an added responsibility: passing along what you have learned to others, especially to young people. But how do you teach Leadership? Effectively? Well, during the years I taught in the MBA program at Saint Louis University, I found that the most valuable lessons I was giving my students did not come from any textbook, and they had nothing to do with business plans, spreadsheets, marketing tools or yearly revenue statements. Instead, the most valuable lessons came from a deeper realm. Let me give you an illuminating example...

When I first approached the MBA team at Saint Louis University about teaching a course on leadership and entrepreneurship, the director asked me for a copy of my syllabus. A syllabus? Don't laugh but I had no idea what a syllabus even was! The lessons I aimed to teach were lessons I had learned from my many years at the top of the business world. The dean of the business school was skeptical about my approach, to say the very least, but he decided to give me a chance.

"To lead, you need to set an example," I told my students on the first day of class. "You have to set standards. You have to show your colleagues—and your competitors—your values and what sets you apart, what makes you the very best in your chosen field."

To drive that message home, I told them about my training at the Culver Military Academy, and about that iron-clad rule about our daily 6 a.m. lineup: You can't be late! My students were grad students, many of them laid-back types coming straight from their B.A. degree and having little or no experience in the rough-and-tumble world of business. And I told them, "Listen, you are all bright, accomplished graduate students, eager to go out into the world of business, and my job is to help you prepare, to show you how to succeed. So in my class, you have to be on time—and preferably a little early. Do you understand?" Then, to drive that message home, I added this warning: "Guess what? If you're late, you get fired! If you're late, I'm not going to have you in my class. Period!"

Well, for the first few weeks of my class, all my students showed up on time, as any serious employer would expect. During the third week, though, one student showed up late—and he had no credible excuse. At once I stopped the class and asked him to step outside the room. If he had some sort of emergency, I would, of course, give him some leeway, as any real-world business manager would. But this young man had no excuse at all. And he offered no apology either. Well, I knew that with that attitude, he would not last five minutes in a serious business organization. So, as I had promised the class in advance, I fired him on the spot. The young man was shocked—and angry! And he went straight to the dean to complain!

The Dean of the Business Program was shocked too. How could I do such a thing? Fire a student? Who does such a thing? Still, I explained my approach, the real-world message that I was intent on sending to the young man and to all the other students, and with that the dean just shook his head, no doubt eager to reach for an aspirin or something far stronger. But guess what? From there, I never heard a word of complaint. And here's the best part of all: from that point forward, no other student was ever late for my class. Not a one! I had sent a powerful message—and the message stuck. And I can only imagine the number of future careers I had saved in the process! Perhaps, through these pages, I can help save a few more! ▪

28

Stay Focused

As entrepreneurs, we have a flood of ideas come to us every single day. It's downright crazy: so many ideas, so many opportunities—let's create this, let's try that, launch this new product, or this new packaging. It's fun, it's energizing, sure, but if you're not careful, a lack of clear, steady focus can be disruptive—and very dangerous for the long-term health of your enterprise.

In this regard, I often think of those race horses known as trotters, the ones who pull carriages and their drivers as they fly around the track. How do they stay focused—and not distracted—throughout the race? The secret: those blinders they wear. Those blinders force the horses to look straight ahead, not from side to side. Total focus. If you want to succeed in business, especially as an entrepreneur, I say be like those trotters, keep those blinders on and charge straight ahead. That's the way to win the race!

But this is not as easy as I make it sound. Everyone has their own "to do list," often with 30 or 40 items on their list, and their daily schedules are often so clogged with tasks and appointments that they barely know where to start, where to focus their energy. I take a different approach. As I plan my days, weeks and months, I have two or three primary goals that I want to achieve for the good of our business. All the rest is secondary. So I try my best to stay focused on those two or three primary goals. I look at so many companies that run into trouble, and often it's because of that one major failure: they got too ambitious, they tried too many things. In sum, they lost their focus. A mistake I urge you to avoid! ▪

Computer Reports

On this same subject of Staying Focused, I want to highlight a villain that we entrepreneurs and business leaders face all the time, a nasty villain that parades as progress: Computer Reports.

Back in the 1970s, when computers first appeared in our family's liquor and wine distribution business, we all stood up and cheered: our new computers helped us track and manage our sales, our operating costs, our inventory, our payroll totals, and our monthly and annual profit and loss totals too. Good-bye typewriters! Computers also facilitated our company correspondence and lessened the loads of our secretaries, accountants, and sales teams. Still, I soon began to see an insidious downside to our reliance on computer power: an ever-rising tide of computer reports. Each week dozens of computer reports were landing on my desk, and I found myself spending hours and hours reading through them—to the point I often felt I was drowning in those reports and being distracted from what to me are far more important aspects of business leadership.

So one day I finally raised my hand and said, "Enough!"

From there, I zoomed in and specified three categories of reports that I needed to follow each week. Three only! The rest I would leave to my staff. In essence, I cleaned out my work-load—and I cleaned out my head in the process! Now, like a doctor looking at a patient's chart, those three reports enabled me to evaluate the health of our company on a week-by-week basis: Accounts Receivable. Inventory. And Cash Flow. It took me only about 15 minutes each week to read those three reports, and I could immediately spot the areas where we needed to do better and often make big changes too. Let me show you the importance of those three reports...

Accounts Receivable. In our wholesale liquor business, the first report I'd view each week was our Accounts Receivable. Almost at a glance I could see 1.) Who's past due? 2.) Who's not paying? And 3.) What's coming due? Also at a glance, I could see the problems we needed to address. Who do we need to call this week to collect our funds? What's the delay? And if I saw a customer who was late week after week, I knew we had to take effective action. Was this fun? Heck, no! But as "Dr. Rubin" can tell you, managing your Accounts Receivable is an essential part of running a healthy business.

Inventory. This was the second computer report I examined each week. By tracking our inventory, I could immediately see which of our products were moving, which were stuck on our shelves, and what new orders we had coming in. In sum, with this one weekly report I could see the health of our sales operation and what sectors of our business—wines, liquors, or other beverages—were really driving our profits and loss. Doctors routinely check your pulse and blood pressure; checking inventory is a comparable task.

The Cash Flow Report. This was the most important report I would receive each week. And I had it boiled down to a single page: How much cash do we have on hand? What are we paying out this week in expenses, wages, and other costs? And against that total, what collections are due this week? Which are past due? Along with Accounts Receivable and Inventory, the Cash Flow Report gave me a fast, reliable summary of what I needed to know to stay on top of our business. All that in about 15 minutes of reading! That's it: Dr. Rubin's three weekly tools for checking your business health!

Now here's the best part: when you become adept at reading those three reports, what happens? Liberation! Suddenly you have more time and energy to devote to collaborating, to innovating, to finding new ideas, and new markets to conquer. Those three reports become your stepping stones to greater business success. And here's the golden lesson at the heart of it:

Long-term success in business—most any business—is built on a happy marriage of the practical and the inspirational. And when company leadership gets bogged down in a daily flood of computer reports, emails, or secondary meetings, guess what? Everybody loses! Creativity suffers. Staff morale declines. And the energy for inspiration and innovation disappears. So here is Dr. Rubin's ultimate advice for you: use those three reports to help you maintain the right balance between the practical and the inspirational, and then sit back and watch your profits—and your spirits—soar! ▪

Human Resource Director

Back in 1972, when I joined my dad's company, most everything about running a small family business like ours was still "old school," especially in the realms of hiring, promoting, and building a team. As I said back in Lesson 1, Dad and Julian B. Venezky, my "Uncle Julian," founded their life-long partnership on a single handshake. Imagine that today!

Still, in 1972 change was coming, big change, and soon I made an important decision, to create a new post: Human Resource Director. At the time, the rule of thumb was that if you had 50 or more employees, you needed an HR Director and we had more than 50. So I made the hire and it proved to be a major step in the evolution of our company. At a stroke, we became far more professional, not just in our hiring process but also in our ability to handle many of the challenges that I saw coming down the road.

Indeed, when our staff level hit 100, I hired a second HR specialist, and that too proved to be a wise move, handling problems that CEOs and presidents have no time to handle. And today our HR teams do far more than recruit candidates and manage our hiring process. They follow the careers of our employees, they monitor their pay and benefits packages, and if an employee chooses to leave us, our HR team interviews them to see why they are leaving and if there are any larger issues that we need to address. Our HR teams also keep our employee handbook up to date, and they carefully monitor any state or federal legislation that might affect our HR policies.

In today's business world, having a quality HR team is an absolute must. So as you build your companies and your dreams, please remember that golden advice from Steve Jobs: "Great things in business are never done by one person. They're done by a team of people." ∎

PART FIVE

BE SMART
ABOUT MONEY

Success is a lousy teacher. It seduces smart people into thinking they can't lose.

▪ BILL GATES ▪

31

Debt Free

My father was extremely careful with money.

As I mentioned, on the very first page of this book, when I joined his company, Dad was deeply proud of two accomplishments: he had no debt in his business life and he had no debt in his personal life. Even with my own love of taking risks, I have always followed my dad's example, and I have made becoming debt-free a top priority, in my business life and my personal life too. And now I want to show you how that commitment has paid off...

When I bought The Republic of Tea, that crazy gamble, I was not swimming in money. Indeed, to buy the company I had to borrow the money. I was fortunate enough that the Southwest Bank in St. Louis believed in me, and they loaned me the money I needed to buy The Republic of Tea. At the start, though, we had a mountain of debt and I had people asking me:

"Ron, how big do you want your company to be? How are you going to build the brand? What is your target for gross revenues?" Those were important questions, sure, but with my dad's hand on my shoulder, guiding my way, my own first question was this: "How soon can we pay off the bank!"

As it turned out, it took me six years, three months, and fifteen days to pay off that debt, and we finally became debt-free in the year 2000. A cause for celebration! And The Republic of Tea has been debt-free ever since. Likewise, when I launched our River Road Family Vineyards and Winery, instead of going to the bank for a loan, I decided to use the money I had saved over 40 years, so that our winery, too, would be debt-free. And we are still debt-free today. And I believe there is a golden lesson here for all aspiring entrepreneurs and business leaders:

Be smart and careful about money! By all means, follow your dreams, pour your hearts and creative talents into exciting new ventures—that's a fabulous strength of our American system! But along the way, be prudent: if you take out a loan to launch your company, be sure to make the required monthly payment. But also try your very best to make a payment against the principal too. Then, much sooner than later, you too can have the relief and the joy of becoming debt-free. A welcome moment indeed!

And there's something more here, another lesson I learned from my dad: we company owners have a lasting obligation to the people we hire. Especially in privately owned companies like ours, we need to assure our staff and the new people we hire that we are providing them with a strong, reliable platform on which to do their work and build their future. In this light, being debt-free is a clear demonstration of our respect and commitment. Indeed, whenever I invite new people to come join our teams, to put their faith and trust in us, I am always proud to say, "Come join us! We're not some chancy start-up venture; we're debt-free and we're built to last!" ∎

32

Fast Pay Makes Fast Friends

One day, as we were building our bottled water business, we took on a new distributor: Better Brands of Atlanta, Inc. The Georgia-based company was run by a man named Bob Bailey and our terms of payment were 15 days. Meaning we would ship cases of Clearly Canadian to Bob and his team and we would then expect full payment within 15 days. That was the standard at the time in the bottled water business. But Bob Bailey broke the mold.

When we sent off our first shipment of Clearly Canadian, just five days after it arrived Bob sent us a check for the full amount due! I was shocked. This was the first time anyone had paid us faster than those 15 days. So right away I called Bob and said, "Thank you, Bob! But I'm curious: why did you pay us before the bill was even due?" And Bob responded with five words that I will never forget: "Fast pay makes fast friends."

Wow! I had never heard that phrase before, but Bob's five words rang true: anytime you can pay somebody fast, you're going to make fast friends. Moreover, inside those five words was an essential truth about long-term business success: in the best transactions, both sides come away happy and convinced their interests are being properly honored and served. No one feels cheated, everything is fair and square, and, above all, you feel these are people you want to work with and build a lasting relationship. Yes, all that flowed to me from Bob Bailey's five golden words.

From that point forward, Fast Pay Makes Fast Friends became a cherished part of our business DNA. In any business, it's important, of course, that your partners and clients have confidence in your integrity and your ability, and it's also important to have contracts that clearly define your services and your obligations. But paying fast is a very tangible way of expressing your gratitude and your commitment to a business relationship, and it can also bring some unexpected dividends. For instance, when we launched our winery, I made sure to pay our grape growers faster than they had ever been paid before. Our growers couldn't believe it! And I believe this really helped strengthen our young enterprise: because our growers knew we were going to pay them faster than anyone else, they went out of their way to make sure we were satisfied and happy. Again, a beautiful win-win!

To me, the moral of this story is clear: if you have the resources, you should take every opportunity to make use of our Fast Pay Makes Fast Friends business practice. In the end, it will pay you great dividends, and it will remind you, time and again, that in the best business relationships, the ones that really last, both sides feel that their needs and desires are being fully honored and served. And that, indeed, is a relationship you can bank on! ∎

33

Estate Planning

At the start of my 50-plus years in business, I tried my best to follow some ancient advice: Hope for the best, but prepare for the worst! I tried my best to follow that guidance both in my business life and my personal life. That said, I was by no means a master at financial planning.

Indeed, when my dad passed away, and I was taking the reins of our company, I did not have a proper will, and I knew very little about trusts or estates, or how best to protect my family's financial assets. Fortunately, though, our local YPO chapter, our Young Presidents' Organization, came to my rescue. One day, as part of their speakers program, the YPO brought in Frank Nitikman, an attorney with the powerhouse firm of McDermott, Will & Emery. And Frank's topic that day was Estate Planning. In his presentation, Frank explained the laws regarding estates, and he explained, in detail, how to set up your own estate and trust. I was impressed. We had about 40 members in our YPO chapter and about 30 of them used Frank for their estate planning. I signed on too—and the man was a godsend!

With Frank's guidance, I created an estate plan, I put my finances in proper order, safe for the future, and what a relief that was for me and our family! Frank also helped me with something else: life insurance. Both whole life and term life. As I will explain in a moment, my term life policy proved to be a blessing after I had my life-threatening heart episode—after that, no life insurance company would be willing to provide me with proper coverage, not at a reasonable cost anyway. These were all invaluable steps to take, and I owe so much to the Illini YPO and to Frank Nitikman! Thank you, Frank!

So my advice to you is simple: Find a quality advisor like Frank to help you with estate planning, trusts, insurance policies, and your other financial tools. Put everything in order—now! You will not regret it, I promise! ∎

34

Term Life Insurance

In my early years in business, most people I knew were choosing to buy "whole life" insurance policies. In the event of their early death, their whole life policies would be a reliable way to provide for their spouses and children. Fine. But when I bought The Republic of Tea—and borrowed a lot of money to do it—I suddenly had an additional worry: if, God forbid, I should die tomorrow, who would pay off my debt to the bank? For guidance, I met with qualified advisors and I decided to take out a "term life" policy. Here's why:

The first virtue I saw in term life was Cost. The rates for a term policy are different now, but the other day I went online to compare the prices of term life policies versus whole life policies. Specifically, I looked at prices for a $10 million term life policy. For a man 40 years old, I found a term policy that would cost $217 a month, about $2,600 a year. For that sum, if the worst happens, your family would receive $10 million dollars—at a rate far below what a $10 million whole life policy would cost you.

The second virtue I saw was Flexibility. Term policies are structured to cover you for a fixed amount of time: 10 years, 20 years, and the like. But here's the beauty of it: as you get older, and your financial obligations change—you pay off your mortgage, college loans, or your business debt—you can restructure your term policy, or even buy another policy providing less coverage. Most whole life policies do not give you that kind of flexibility.

The third virtue I saw was Peace of Mind, and for me that was the clincher. With a term life policy, if I passed away tomorrow, Pam and our two children would be well covered—with enough funds to pay off that loan from Southwest Bank too. Done! And thanks to my term life policy, I sleep much better at night. My ultimate advice here? Be smart. Carefully evaluate your family's needs. Get expert advice. And then make your best decision. ▪

Private Physicians

As I put my finances in order—and enjoyed the peace of mind that came with it—I also looked for ways to assure that, going forward, my family had the best possible health care... at a manageable price. I investigated several options and then I made my decision: I hired a private physician.

My reasons here were several. For one, as we all have seen, our health care system in America has changed dramatically in recent years—and not entirely for the better. Today, in big cities and small, a patient in need of care can wait days, weeks, or even months to see the right specialist or to have a non-urgent surgery or other treatment at a leading hospital. In some cases, the wait time is not only excessive, it can actually threaten the life of the patient. And many hospitals in remote areas are simply shutting down.

In my case, when I had my heart episode, I was extremely lucky: I had the best possible care—and I had it fast! Still, traveling regularly as Pam and I do, between St. Louis, California and other places, and with my heart issues still a concern, I felt that hiring a private physician would be the best solution for our family, giving us ongoing care we could always trust.

After a careful search, I found a skilled, very caring private physician in California, and he charges an annual fee of $3,500. Other physicians charge $5,000 or more. Either way, I view this as a smart investment. Our doctor knows us well, and he has all of our medical records right at his fingertips. And when any of us is in need, we get help—*fast!* No waiting. I have his office number, I have his cell number. And he is the anchor of all of our health care needs. If I have a heart twinge, he has a quality specialist in his directory, no matter where we are. If Pam has an ache or pain, it's the same: she gets quality care and she gets it fast. There are other good options, of course, but for me it's a tremendous relief to have that kind of care always so close to hand. ▪

36

Dollar Cost Averaging/
Equity vs. Fixed

Now, in this same spirit, I set out to build a much stronger financial future for our family. But how to do that? Invest in stocks and bonds or in houses, buildings, or other long-term assets? And how best to balance those investments? Well, many of the answers here came to me from a remarkable man named John C. Bogle, a giant in the history of investment.

Like Sam Walton, the founder of Walmart and Sam's Club, John Bogle knew a thing or two about financial hardship. He came of age at the height of The Great Depression and it hit his family smack in the face: they lost all their money and their home in Montclair, New Jersey. With all that, John's father sunk into alcoholism and his parents soon divorced.

But John and his twin brother David were determined to bounce back and succeed. They both earned scholarships to Blair Academy, in Warren County, New Jersey, and there John showed a particular gift for mathematics and computations. After he graduated from Blair, cum laude, John entered Princeton University, and there he found his true calling: economics and investment strategies. After graduating from Princeton, magna cum laude, in 1951, John was hired by Walter L. Morgan, the founder of the Wellington Fund, a highly respected investment group. In 1970, brilliant as he was, John succeeded Walter Morgan as the chairman of Wellington's mutual funds group. In the world of investment, John C. Bogle was a star!

Then it happened...

As chairman, Bogle approved a risky merger and the decision blew up in his face. The Wellington board promptly fired him. Still, stunned by that failure, what did John Bogle do? Hang his head and give up? Oh, no! John learned the necessary lessons and charged right back into action. "The great thing about that mistake," he later wrote, "was that I learned a lot." From there, John founded his own company, The Vanguard Group, and he built it into one of the most respected companies in the world of investment. In 1999, Fortune magazine named John Bogle as "one of the four investment giants of the twentieth century." Wow! Naturally, I had to read all about him—and what golden lessons he brought me!

John wrote several acclaimed books on how to wisely invest your money, and in his seminal work, *John Bogle on Investing*, he introduced me to an investment strategy called "dollar cost averaging." I had no idea what that was, but as a young guy getting ready to buy some stocks or mutual funds, I was eager to learn, and through his book John set me on a path that quickly proved its worth. Here is what he recommended:

Set aside a specific sum of money to invest each month, say $1,000, then buy one stock or one mutual fund every month—regardless if the market is going up or down. Just be consistent month after month. This strategy is what John calls "dollar cost averaging." Some months your $1,000 will buy you more shares, some months it will buy you fewer—it all depends on the market at that moment. But with that strategy, you're not trying to guess the market's ups and downs. Instead, just by staying steady and consistent, you will, over the long-term, get a reliable return on your investment. I followed John's strategy, and it has worked very well for me.

To optimize your "dollar cost averaging" strategy, John then added another layer of wisdom: balance your equity investments with your fixed investments, using a formula based on your age. Here's the gist of it: if, for instance, you are aged 70, John recommends that you have 70 percent of your money in fixed investments, such as real estate or government bonds, and 30 percent in equity investments, such as the stock market. If, on the other hand, you are 30 years old, it's just the reverse: John recommends that you put 30 percent of your money in fixed investments and 70 percent in stocks. And when you're 50, John urges you to balance your investments at 50-50. Again, I followed John's advice, with very happy results.

Today I work with Katherine B. Lintz, a brilliant financial planner in St. Louis, and when we sit down to talk, she knows what my priorities are. Kathy knows what percentage of my holdings I want in fixed assets, and what percentage I want in equity, meaning stocks. As an experienced financial advisor and the founder of her own firm, Matter Family Office, Kathy serves as the quarterback of all my personal financial planning, and together we hold to John Bogle's basic investment formula. With wonderful results! In recent years, the market has had huge ups and downs, but my investments have remained steady and secure—and for that I owe very grateful bows to Kathy Lintz and to John Bogle, my personal king of investment strategy! ■

Personal Financial Statement

Today as I write these pages, and as I think about all the lessons I've learned over the years, one word keeps popping to mind: "Clarity."

In my business life, over and over I saw the importance of Clarity. Of clear, compelling Mission Statements. Clear budgets, clear Profit and Loss Statements, clear Cash Flow reports, and more. In business, those tools keep you on track and help you safeguard the future of your business. But what about your personal finances? How can you best build and safeguard your personal financial future? Here I often felt I had no Clarity at all!

So one day I sat down with Mike Patterson, my CPA, and I said to him, "Mike, each year we assemble all kinds of statements, for my taxes, my mortgage, for our family expenses over the year, but I don't have a reliable scorecard, one sure way to have everything laid out clearly before me."

Well, right there Mike helped me create the exact tool I needed: a Personal Financial Statement. And the result was clear as day. On the statement, we list **Assets** on one side and **Liabilities** on the other. On the Assets side, we include cash in the bank, stocks and bonds, mutual funds, my 401K plan, and my real estate holdings. On the Liabilities side, we list my mortgage, any auto loans, my tuition obligations, and all the rest. The bottom line? By listing my Total Assets against my Total Liabilities, I could clearly see my financial health and what I needed to do to improve it: namely Grow my Assets and Reduce my Liabilities.

From there, with my Personal Financial Statement in hand, I was able to zero in on those goals, track my progress, and bring those Liabilities right down to zero! And I have relied on my Personal Financial Statement ever since. Another golden lesson I am happy to share with you now! ▪

WHEN
TROUBLES
COME

Adversity can be a
magnificent teacher.

▪ RON RUBIN ▪

Tragedy: Be Prepared

Let me tell you now about a wonderful man named George Phillips.

For more than a decade, George was a cherished colleague of ours at The Republic of Tea. He was a top-quality systems guy at our plant in Nashville, Illinois, and we gave him a special title that honored his skills: "Minister of Smooth Operations." I loved George, we all did.

George lived in Mt. Vernon, Illinois, about 25 minutes away from our plant, and one morning, as he drove to work, something terrible happened. Nobody knows why, but less than a mile from the turn-in to our plant, George's car suddenly veered into the oncoming lane and was slammed head-on by a tractor-trailer. George was killed on the spot. It was stunning, a tragedy of the most wrenching kind.

I was shocked and heartsick; we all were. People were crying inside our plant and wondering how this could have happened. George was a skilled driver; was he drowsy?

Did he have some sort of seizure? Was he reaching for his phone? No one knew and that made it all the worse. To this day, no one has a clue what really caused the deadly crash.

How, as a company leader, can you prepare for a tragedy like this? I had no idea. I had never been through anything like this. And I'm not sure any company can adequately prepare for this sort of sudden emotional blow. What we did right away, though, was hire a crisis consultant. On his advice, we set up grief counseling sessions for our entire staff, and we established a crisis communication team to help us move forward. And the guiding lesson here was now smack in our face: Bad things happen—Be Prepared!

But how do you prepare? In our case, we put together an 80-page handbook, our "Crisis Management Plan," and it proved to be a very effective tool. One section sets forth a "Crisis Response Checklist"—the key steps to follow in a crisis. Another section teaches our staff how to prepare our facilities for future crises, and another sets up a call tree, prioritizing who to call first in an emergency: police, fire, medical teams and more. Another section sets out "News Media Do's and Don'ts," and how to manage social media in the event of an emergency. All this is essential information, of course, and I urge you, as company leaders, to create your own Crisis Management Plans, tailored to your specific needs and locales.

Today my heart still aches over the loss of George Phillips. He was a cherished and admired member of our team at The Republic of Tea. Still, in death as in life, George brought us a golden lesson for your business and your life: Bad things happen. Be Prepared! ∎

Mistakes

As I matured in the business world, handling the bad with the good, my thoughts often returned to my first two mentors: my dad and my Uncle Julian. And I still treasure the advice I got from both of them: "Listen, Ron, you're going to make mistakes. That's just a given. Mistakes are a normal part of business—and of life. So accept it. Be ready for it. Then learn the relevant lessons, move on, and don't make the same mistake twice!"

That is advice I have honored ever since. In our start-up years at The Republic of Tea, for instance, when we were watching every dollar we spent, and making mistakes left and right, I came up with a novel idea: to actually budget for mistakes. So in our budget's expense category we put in a line item called "Make Mistakes," with a figure of $50,000. And the novel idea worked! When we did make the inevitable mistake, and it cost us say, $10,000, that budget item helped take the sting out of it. Later on, as our company grew—and we became more adept at managing it—I stopped the practice, but it did help us get through those dicey start-up years.

For every entrepreneur and business leader, my message to you is simple: Expect mistakes. Prepare for them. Learn from them. As Nick Saban and other championship coaches remind us, every team and every player will experience moments of triumph and moments of defeat. That's a given. So the ultimate test is your inner strength and resolve, and your ability to turn your mistakes and setbacks into incentives for greater learning and growth. To my mind, the basketball legend Michael Jordan expressed it perfectly:

"I've missed more than 9000 shots in my career. I've lost almost 300 games. Twenty six times, I've been trusted to take the game-winning shot and I've missed it. I've failed over and over and over again in my life. And that is why I succeed." ∎

Lowlights

That's a golden lesson from Michael Jordan.

But how, as a leader, do you inspire your people, in the good times and bad? In the face of adversity, how do you motivate your teams to keep working hard, to keep right on learning, and keep right on striving to be the very best in their field? In sum, how do you teach your people to turn life's inevitable setbacks into lasting triumphs, the way Michael Jordan and so many other champions learned to do?

These questions are crucial to long-term success in business and in life. And, as you have no doubt seen, in good times and bad, my gut instinct as a leader is to stay positive and upbeat, to celebrate the strengths of our people, and to highlight our efforts to be good partners in our communities and our industries. That's just my instinct: Emphasize The Positive. One day, though, I learned a crucial lesson, about the virtues of showcasing not just your highlights but also your "Lowlights." Let me tell you the story...

This lesson came to me from a book I mentioned earlier, *Trillion Dollar Coach*, about Bill Campbell, the celebrated football and life coach who later became the trusted mentor to so many Silicon Valley leaders and creators. Like every successful coach, Bill knew that his teams were going to experience thrilling victories, but also agonizing defeats. So in his training sessions, he always advised his followers at Google, Apple and elsewhere to openly acknowledge their shortcomings and failures, their "Lowlights." As Bill Campbell helped me understand, openly admitting your mistakes or shortcomings is a mark of courage and conviction—and those are essential qualities of leadership, for building a strong and resilient team. Fabulous!

For me, Mr. Positive, this was exceptionally good advice, on a par, I can see now, with being prepared for tragedy, as I learned from the death of our friend George Phillips. Since then, I always put Bill Campbell's advice into practice in our reports and our company meetings. No more speeches or presentations where we speak only of our highlights; if we mess up or we have setbacks, we admit it, we confront it, then we learn the relevant lessons and move forward, stronger, wiser, and with our credibility intact.

Bill Campbell loved coaching, he loved inspiring others, and he especially loved working with people who had the vision, the guts, and the raw determination to become the very best in their fields. I learned so much from this man, about "Heads Held High" and "Lowlights" and so much more. And at the very end of *Trillion Dollar Coach*, the authors cite a line from Bill Campbell that I cherish and am happy to share with you now: "If you've been blessed, be a blessing." Amen! Bless you, Bill Campbell! ▪

Pivot

Speaking of Lowlights, Covid for us was among the worst.

As you know, the outbreak of the COVID-19 virus caused huge trouble for the entire world. It hit America in January of 2020 and by mid-March panic was sweeping the nation. The federal government and public health officials in every state and town across the country put in place emergency measures. Masks were ordered. Schools closed, restaurants closed, public transport was curtailed, and by September of 2020, just eight months later, the Covid virus had already claimed 95,000 lives across America. And worse was soon to come: the Covid pandemic wound up killing 1.1 million people here in America and millions more around the world. Awful, awful!

The Covid crisis hit our young winery too. Hard. We launched our dream venture in December of 2011, and in 2014 we brought out our first wines. At that stage, our aims were modest and our strategy was clear: we would start our business with "on premise" sales, meaning sales to nearby restaurants and bistros. No Costcos, no Total Wine & More. We didn't have the grape supply for that. Or the staff. Or the brand. At that stage, we had two primary wines to sell: a Russian River Pinot Noir and a Russian River Chardonnay. At first, we struggled and argued over what name to give our wines and our brand, but for starters we decided on a simple name for both: "Ron Rubin Wines." At that early stage, that was the best we had.

In our first years in business, we did well with our "on premise" strategy. The restaurants we targeted bought our wines and sold them by the glass and for "in-house pours," for whole tables of guests. I was encouraged. But then Covid hit. And much of American life immediately ground to a halt. In our corner of Northern California, few people dared go out to eat. Scores of our client restaurants closed. Goodbye, wine sales! Goodbye, dream!

So right there we went into crisis mode. We re-examined everything we were doing. Our "on premise" strategy. Our product lines. And, like every company in America, we struggled to assess what impact the Covid pandemic would have on the future of our business. Could we even survive? With so much at stake, we spent three solid months trying to figure out what to do. Finally, in early July of 2020, we made our decision: Pivot!

With that, we shifted our strategy, immediately, from "on premise" to "off premise" sales. Meaning from restaurants to wine shops. This was a radical shift, but we had to make it. So many restaurants had closed their doors, but most wine shops were still open for business. And doing good business too. Many wine shops, in big cities especially, were taking orders by phone, then delivering their wines right to your door, with deliverymen masked every step of the way. Target and other chains also featured home deliveries. The result? Our pivot succeeded—and it kept us alive.

We faced a similar crisis at The Republic of Tea. Back in 1997, we had brought out something new: a glass-bottled tea, and it became a big hit with what we in the trade call "white table cloth restaurants." Soon we were selling thousands and thousands of cases of our glass-bottled teas. A huge success! But then Covid hit. Countless restaurants across the country immediately closed, while others radically reduced their staffs and their seating spaces. Sales of our bottled teas plummeted. What to do? Pivot!

First, we changed our sales focus. So many restaurants were closing or cutting back, but families still had a constant need: trips to the grocery store. So grocery stores and chains now became our focus. To make the shift, from the "white tablecloth" crowd to everyday consumers, we cut the size of our tea bottles from 16.9 ounces to 12 ounces, and we lowered the price too. The result? Our pivot worked—and it saved our business. And the entire Covid crisis crowned for me a golden lesson: Adversity can be a magnificent teacher—if you have the skills and the resilience to handle it! ▪

PART SEVEN

FOR THE GREATER GOOD

I want to put a ding in the universe.

■ STEVE JOBS ■

42

Giving Back

Let me share with you a little secret.

As you have seen throughout these pages, I love the worlds of business and entrepreneurship. I love the challenges, I love the excitement of innovating, collaborating, and educating, and I love sharing with our customers the very best that our vision, our talents, and our teams can produce. And I love, too, working with like-minded people, people who love sharing their lives and their dreams and their skills with us, and who are often the very best in their chosen fields. Who could ask for more?

Still, as I look back today, I find that my deepest and most lasting satisfactions have come from a very different source: from Giving Back, from serving our communities, from working for a greater good, and from our efforts to make this world a better place. Put simply, Giving Back feels great, and it brings my family and me satisfactions that reach far beyond the world of business, and reach into a much deeper place inside each of us.

I'm thinking here of the satisfactions I have had from creating The Ron Rubin School for Entrepreneurship at Culver Academies. I'm thinking of our campaigns to find cures for breast cancer and prostate cancer. I'm thinking of our Blue Bin bottle initiative and our other efforts in support of environmental protection and sustainable agriculture. I'm thinking, too, about our support for the wine programs at U.C. Davis and Sonoma State University, and about teaching MBA students at Saint Louis University. A few pages ahead, I will tell you about two other initiatives that I hold dear: our campaign to become a Certified B Corporation, and a special program we launched, "Trained For Saving Lives," to help people suddenly struck down by a life-threatening heart episode. As you will see, these are two of the most needed—and most satisfying—things I have ever done.

I am also delighted and proud to report that our two wonderful children, Julie and Todd, are also deeply committed to Giving Back, through education, philanthropic causes, and community service.

Julie and her husband, Jay Liberman, live in Plano, Texas, a suburb of Dallas, along with their children, Sally and Ray. For many years, Julie has been an active supporter and a board member of the Jewish Family Service in Dallas. Innovation is in her DNA. In 2011, Julie and two colleagues, Cathy Glick and Beverly Rossel, launched a successful fund-raising and PR effort for JFS: an annual "Diaper Shower," to provide clean diapers and sanitary wipes to needy families throughout the area. The program has been providing much needed help to struggling families ever since.

"Parents are struggling more than ever to afford diapers and wipes for their babies," says Cathy Barker, JFS President and CEO. "Inflation is hitting everyone—across the board—especially those who are already living outside their means." Julie agrees and sees the need as urgent:

"There are parents today reusing diapers or waiting to change their children until the end of the day, to stretch whatever supplies they have. It's not out of neglect. Sometimes there just is no choice. Our annual Diaper Shower provides a necessity for those in immediate need." Over the years, the program has provided needy families with more than two million diapers!

Julie's husband, Jay Liberman, a wealth management consultant in Dallas, is also devoted to Giving Back. He and Julie have both been active supporters of the Jewish Federation of Greater Dallas, and of the Aaron Family Jewish Community Center. For the Aaron Family JCC, Julie and Jay chaired a campaign that raised over $500,000 to build a safe, natural, outdoor environment for kids to explore and enjoy. A community effort good for the heart and good for the soul. Bravo, bravo!

Our son Todd honors the same values and ideals, and the same Rubin family commitment to education and community service. Todd majored in architecture at Syracuse University. After graduation, he worked for an architectural design firm for three years. But in 2007, eager for wider challenges, Todd joined us at The Republic of Tea. He started as our "Minister of Commerce" for the East and then the Southeast, and he soon mastered all the elements of running a successful family business. In 2011, Todd became our "Minister of Evolution," and he moved west to take charge of our new corporate headquarters in Larkspur, California, and he has done wonders to build our company into an industry giant.

Today our commitment to Giving Back is deeply woven into the DNA of our family company, The Republic of Tea. Indeed, the company offers tea lovers 350 different varieties of premium teas and natural herbs, and all of our teas are produced in accordance with the highest standards of quality, environmental protection, and corporate social responsibility. To learn more about our sense of mission and our commitment to Giving Back, please visit our website, republicoftea.com.

Also on our website you will see the full extent of our campaign to promote education and positive social change around the world. Over the years, we have forged alliances with Japan House, Sri Lanka's Women of Tea, The Dr. Marnie Rose Foundation, Keep Memory Alive, Homeward Bound of Marin, The Whole Planet Foundation, Room To Read, Seeds of Learning, The American Red Cross, The Prostate Cancer Foundation, and The Susan G. Komen Foundation and its efforts to find a cure for breast cancer. Innovate. Educate. Inspire. Yes, it's all sealed now in our DNA, and I assure you that nothing feels as deeply rewarding as Giving Back. ▪

43

Make A Difference Day

Along with our family initiatives in the field of giving, we work hard to encourage others to Give Back to worthy causes. To that end, at both The Republic of Tea and at our River Road Family Vineyards and Winery we have a tradition that we honor and hold dear: our "Make A Difference Day."

With this, we offer our employees two full days a year—at full pay—to work for a non-profit cause of their choosing. We do not support working for a specific political party, or any specific religious group. Instead, we encourage our employees to find and support a cause that has special meaning for themselves, their families, or their communities.

This is not a half-hearted effort. As we state in our Strategic Plans, we encourage 100 percent participation in our Make A Difference Days. To that end, we carefully review our employees proposed organizations to help, and then we track their participation. Many of our employees have chosen to help organizations doing cancer research or helping cancer victims in their times of need. Other employees work with non-profit organizations devoted to protecting the environment, or helping people with HIV or with special needs. Many of the employees at our winery in Sonoma County actively support local groups that stock food banks and take care of the homeless in our communities. Work that's good for the heart, and good for the soul.

Our Make A Difference Days highlight the ideals and values that we honor as companies and as a family: Give Back. Help others. Work for the greater good. For the greater good of our communities, our environment, and our planet too. And for our teams and our family too, our underlying message here is clear: lead a life of meaning and purpose, lead a life where at the close of every day you feel you have truly Made A Difference. ∎

44

Medjet Assist

I am one lucky guy.

When I had my terrible heart scare, that "ventricular tachycardia," several different teams of specialists stepped up and saved my life. In my eyes, these men and women are true heroes, doing work that is vital to our communities and to our country, and I am determined to help advance their efforts. So right here, let me tell you my heart story in much greater detail.

This was the summer of 2009, and Pam and I were spending a few months at our condo in Tiburon, California, so we could be close to our son Todd and close to the California offices of The Republic of Tea. Well, on the morning of September 6th, 2009, Todd and I met for breakfast and, as we were walking back to our condo, I suddenly felt a strange sensation. At first, it just felt like my arm was falling asleep. But then—

wham!—a series of shocks began ripping through my entire body, to the point where I felt paralyzed and couldn't walk another step.

Right away Todd swung into action. He called 911, an ambulance came minutes later and sped me to the nearby Marin General Hospital, where the doctors in the ER found my heart was racing out of control. Right away they hooked me up to a high-tech marvel called an AED, short for Automated External Defibrillator. Right away, the AED sent electric shock waves into my heart and those shock waves soon brought my heart rate down to a safer level. Whew! Luck was with me: that AED saved my life! What a fabulous tool that is! But the crisis wasn't over: the heart specialists at Marin General Hospital said I still needed emergency surgery.

Right there I had only one desire: to go back home to St. Louis for the emergency surgery. The ER doctors in Marin were terrific, but our family doctors were all back in St. Louis, I had great faith in the staff at the Barnes-Jewish Hospital, and our primary residence was there too. Still, I was in no shape to just go to a nearby airport and hop on the earliest flight. No way! And I knew I would need emergency care all the way back to St. Louis, with a medical team onboard monitoring my condition. But what would that cost?

Todd was with me in the ER, and I asked him to make some urgent calls about hiring a private jet. Todd did, and he soon came back with the answer: an emergency flight back home would cost $60,000! Yikes! Now what? Then suddenly I remembered a program called Medjet Assist.

Years before, I had read about Medjet in Fortune magazine, and now I said to Todd, "Get me my wallet!" And sure enough, in my wallet I found my Medjet card, dating back several years. I had never used it, but I kept it there in case of emergency, along with my AAA card. Now, with one call to Medjet, Todd confirmed that I had paid the yearly dues—all of $300—and on the spot, Medjet stepped up and arranged for a special medical jet to fly us from the private airport in nearby Napa directly back to St. Louis. The plane would have nurses onboard, plus extensive medical equipment should I need it. And the price for all this emergency care? Zero! Not a dime. The entire cost was covered under the Medjet plan. Wow!

To my relief, the Medjet Assist crews and system worked perfectly, and I have now put my whole family and many of my staff and advisors into the Medjet program as well. At an annual cost of only $350 per person! Talk about a lesson learned! And, of course, I am now a fervent supporter of Medjet Assist and its important life-saving mission. My advice to you now: check it out! Your life could depend on it!

Still, the Medjet teams were just the beginning of the story. Listen to what happened next... ∎

45

CPR, AEDs

As soon as we arrived safely back in St. Louis, thanks to Medjet, I was rushed to the Barnes-Jewish Hospital for emergency surgery, to be done the following Monday. Would my life be forever changed? Would I even survive the surgery? Laying in that hospital bed, I had no clue. None. And the smell of death was right in my nostrils.

Thankfully, the doctors at the Barnes-Jewish Hospital were terrific: I survived the surgery, and what an education I got in the process! Back in the ER in California, doctors had used that AED defibrillator to save my life, and now, during the operation in St. Louis, my team of doctors opened my chest and inserted another type of defibrillator, an ICD, short for Implantable Cardioverter Defibrillator. My doctors placed the ICD just under my skin, with thin wires leading straight into my heart. From there, the ICD monitors and controls my heart rate on a constant basis. If my heart starts to race, and reaches a level of 145 beats per minute, the ICD sends small shocks into my heart to slow it down. And if my heart rate should jump to a life-threatening 160 beats per minute, the ICD sends in stronger shock waves, to bring my heart rate back down to a safe level. Just like the AED that had saved my life in California, my new ICD has been a godsend; since it was installed back in 2009, my ICD has saved my life five different times! I bow in gratitude...

All this, of course, sent me into action...

As I explained earlier, this brush with death was a true awakening—one that transformed my life's priorities—and it sent Pam and me off on a search to find our own stretch of heaven in California Wine Country, a place with vineyards of our own, a place to make fine wines for all of us to enjoy. At the same time, this brush with death also set me off on a much larger mission: to help others who might suffer a sudden life-threatening cardiac arrest. As a first step, I established CPR training sessions for our teams at The Republic of Tea and our River Road Family Vineyards and Winery. With that CPR training, I wanted our team to be able to treat, right on the spot, any employee or visitor who might suddenly suffer a serious heart episode. As I had learned earlier, Bad Things Happen. Be Prepared!

As a next step, I launched a much wider program called "Trained For Saving Lives." My primary goal here was to help all of Sonoma County's 450 wineries be equipped to handle life-threatening heart emergencies. In my eyes, the need was urgent: California Wine Country gets millions of visitors every single year, with people often visiting wineries that are located far away from towns or emergency services. So wineries need to be prepared—and our Trained for Saving Lives program is designed to do just that. For help, we joined forces with the American Red Cross to provide winery employees with CPR training, and with the ZOLL Medical Corporation to supply those life-saving AEDs. Be prepared! Be equipped! And the result?

Today I am happy to report that through our Trained for Saving Lives program, we have trained and equipped more than 400 wineries in Sonoma County, and several wineries in neighboring Napa Valley have also joined the cause. And so has a winery in Colorado. In all, we have brought our CPR and AED training to more than 2,000 winery employees. I'm thrilled! We're making a difference! But we need to do more, much more...

According to the latest medical statistics, every single day across America 1,000 people or more suffer a sudden, life-threatening cardiac emergency. Yes, 1,000 people every day! That's 365,000 people a year! And the majority of those people do not survive the attack. Most don't even make it to the hospital for the emergency care they need. But our Trained for Saving Lives program can make a huge difference and save thousands of those lives every single year. And I am pleased to report that the issue of sudden cardiac arrest is now gaining prominent national attention, thanks to three amazing stories that I am happy to share with you now... ▪

46

Saving Lives

Monday Night Football, a cherished American tradition.

And on the Monday night of January 2nd, 2023, millions of football fans gathered in front of their TVs for the national broadcast of a major NFL contest: the Buffalo Bills versus the Cincinnati Bengals. But what happened that night was of a significance reaching far beyond the realm of football.

In the first quarter, Damar Hamlin, a strong, healthy, 24-year-old safety for the Buffalo Bills, made what appeared to be a routine tackle of the Bengals receiver Tee Higgins. After the play, Hamlin stood up, but after just two steps—*bang!*—he collapsed. What happened? Nobody knew!

Trainers rushed to Hamlin's side and, diagnosing the problem as cardiac arrest, they immediately administered CPR and managed to revive his heart. But the drama was far from over. Hamlin was then strapped onto a stretcher and rushed to the

University of Cincinnati Medical Center, for emergency tests and treatment. Still, with everyone in the stadium watching in shock and confusion, and countless millions watching it all on TV, NFL officials suspended the game for an hour, and then they stopped the game altogether and postponed it indefinitely. With good reason.

"It was a nightmare," said Joe Buck, ESPN's announcer. "It certainly was nothing that anyone is ever prepared for. You have all that hype and buildup, and everyone can't wait to watch this matchup, and in the snap of a finger it's completely different. Football just goes out the window."

Indeed. And as doctors soon discovered, Damar Hamlin had suffered a rare heart disturbance known as *commotio cordis*, Latin for "agitation of the heart." This condition, doctors say, is triggered by a severe blow to the chest, as happened when Hamlin tackled Tee Higgins. The condition was first observed in the 1700s, but it became better known in the 1990s. Still, this event was seen as a first in the history of the National Football League.

And what had saved Damar Hamlin's life? What had those trainers used to revive his heart? The same amazing device that had saved my own life: an AED, an Automated External Defibrillator. Right there on the field, the trainers had used an AED to jolt Damar's heart and calm it down to a safer level. Within a week, Damar was recovering well, and he was moved from the intensive care unit at the University of Cincinnati Medical Center to a special heart unit at the Buffalo General Medical Center. And just two days later, his doctors in Buffalo declared Damar fit enough to return to his normal life, on and off the field. A happy ending to a terrible scare, all played out on national TV. Damar's teammates were relieved and thrilled, and Damar showed his appreciation with effusive posts on social media, thanking his trainers and doctors. The national press followed the story closely, often highlighting the life-saving role of the AED, and for me all this underscored the importance of our Trained for Saving Lives program.

Then there was Bronny James.

Bronny, the son of NBA superstar LeBron James, also owes a huge thank you to his trainers and to the life-saving power of the AED. On July 24th, 2023, Bronny was working hard during a basketball practice session at his university, USC. He was strong, fit, and only 18 years old, but in the middle of practice Bronny suddenly collapsed right there on the court. What happened? Nobody was sure. But USC trainers rushed to his side, found that Bronny's heart was racing out of control, and they immediately used an AED to jolt and calm his racing heart. According to the American Heart Association, some 95 percent of sudden cardiac arrest victims never even make it to the hospital. But thanks to his trainers and that AED, Bronny did.

From the gym, Bronny was rushed to Cedars-Sinai Medical Center in Los Angeles, for emergency treatment. Over the following three days, with his family in shock and fearing for his life, Bronny's doctors discovered that the young man had a congenital heart defect. A defect no one had spotted before. Happily, the doctors were able to successfully fix the defect, and Bronny was soon on his way to a full recovery. A fabulous outcome, thanks to his doctors, his trainers, and, again, the power of the AED defibrillator. And just think of all the high school and college teams across America that don't have access to that kind of life-saving care. We need to address that!

And that brings me now to our own Dave Shrum.

Dave was born and raised in St. Louis, and after college he started his career as a production manager in a cream cheese company headquartered in St. Louis. Four years later, Dave joined our team at The Republic of Tea, in our plant in Nashville, Illinois, working again as a production manager. And Dave was terrific. At that early stage, we had six production lines, and he managed our production staff, our scheduling, and all of our maintenance needs. Soon we expanded to 17 production lines, and Dave guided us every step of the way. Dave is a modest, very capable guy, with a wife and two kids, and he has been an anchor of our operation for almost two decades.

Back in high school, in a swimming class, Dave learned an essential skill: CPR. That stands for Cardiopulmonary Resuscitation, meaning what to do if someone's heart stops beating, or it beats too weakly to circulate enough blood to the brain and other vital organs. The basic CPR procedure is this: if someone is hit with a cardiac disorder, place the person flat on his or her back, then with both hands centered on their chest, press down firmly with 30 compressions, allowing the chest to return to its normal position after each compression. After 30 compressions, switch to mouth-to-mouth resuscitation, holding the person's nose shut and forcing in your breath to unblock the airway and pour fresh oxygen into the victim's system. CPR works. CPR saves lives. For decades, the American Red Cross and schools and health organizations across the country have given CPR training to anyone who wants it. And they have saved countless lives in the process.

Saving Lives! That is why, after my own heart scare, I made CPR training a requirement for our staffs at The Republic of Tea and our River Road Family Vineyards and Winery. And we provide our teams with CPR refresher classes too. In Dave Shrum's case, he had a refresher course in June of 2020 and, as it turned out, the timing could not have been better...

On August 13th of 2020, just two months later, Dave was out on the golf course with a buddy of his, Steve Beimfoher, the owner of a popular restaurant in Nashville, Illinois, and they were having a grand old time. It was hot that August day, stifling hot, and Steve was coughing a lot. "Don't worry," he assured Dave. "It's just my old asthma kicking up..."

At 1 p.m., on the 14th hole, far away from the clubhouse, Dave and Steve walked up to the green. "My ball was on the green, and Steve's was on the fringe," Dave recalls now. "Then, all of a sudden, I heard Steve just flop backwards. He plunged straight back and I knew right away what it was: a heart attack. I ran to the golf cart, grabbed my cellphone, and called 911."

Right away Dave told the dispatcher what had happened and asked for immediate medical help. Then, with his phone beside him, on speaker, he went to work. "I started CPR," Dave says. "Thirty compressions. Then two breaths. Thirty compressions, then two breaths. And I told the dispatcher to call the golf course, tell them where I'm at, and to have someone on hand to show the paramedics exactly where I am."

Dave performed CPR steadily for 15 minutes as he waited for the paramedics to arrive. "In training, they always tell you, Don't stop! And once or twice, I thought he was gone," Dave says. "But I just kept going. And the dispatcher did a great job; she kept motivating me, encouraging me, and assuring me the paramedics were on their way."

By the time the paramedics arrived and took over, and then rushed Steve to the hospital, Dave was drenched in sweat—and exhausted. But he had saved his buddy's life. Afterwards, the doctors told him that Steve had suffered a type of heart attack so deadly it's called "The Widow-Maker." Yikes! And there was an added element here too: all this happened during the worst of the Covid crisis—a time when many people trained in CPR were unwilling to give mouth-to-mouth resuscitation. "I knew the risks," Dave says now. "But Steve was a friend, so I said, what the heck, I'll do it."

Today, that "Widow-Maker" is behind them, and Steve Beimhofer is alive and well. In fact, Steve and Dave Shrum have lunch together every Thursday, not far from our plant in Nashville. At first, modest guy that he is, Dave didn't tell anyone at the plant about what had happened. But when word did get out, the American Red Cross stepped right up and gave Dave its prestigious Presidential Award, in honor of his courage and skills in saving a life. Bravo! And the ensuing press coverage really helped our cause. In a truly unforgettable way, Dave's heroic story validated our required CPR training and our Trained for Saving Lives program too.

I applaud Dave Shrum. And I applaud Damar Hamlin and Bronny James too. Their three stories carry a message of great hope, hope for the estimated 1,000 people who are hit by a cardiac emergency crisis every single day in America. And the message here is this: We can help! We can save lives! Thanks to our Trained for Saving Lives program, and the generous support we receive from the American Red Cross and Zoll Medical, with their AEDs, we have the tools and the knowhow to save thousands and thousands of lives every single year. So, to all the business leaders across this great country of ours, I say this: Come help! Come join the cause! Together we can put our own ding in the universe! ■

Your Time is Limited

Writing about Bronny James and Damar Hamlin gives me the chills.

Bronny was just 18 years old when he collapsed on that gym floor, and Damar was only 24 when he suddenly collapsed on that football field. Both young men were star athletes, physically fit, mentally fit, and training hard, every single day, working, striving to be the very best they can be.

Then—*wham!*—they went down, their hearts choking, their minds reeling, and neither of them knew what the next moments might bring.

Writing about them now throws me right back onto that bed at the Barnes-Jewish Hospital in St. Louis, waiting for the surgeons to open my chest and figure out what the hell was the matter—and if they could fix it.

I don't know either Bronny or Damar, but I do know this: when these two fine young men regained some strength and got up from their hospital beds, they were filled with gratitude, and filled with a stark awareness of the fragility of life, of just how precious every single day and every hour can be.

And there are golden lessons here for all of us. Whether you're 18, or 24, or 60 years old, as I was when I had my heart scare, no one can be sure what tomorrow might bring, or even the next hour. Sooner or later, life throws all of us nasty setbacks and hardships; that's just a given. That's how we grow. So be ready! Be prepared! And I say this to you: Be bold! Be brave! Live life to the full! Build your dreams, and build them now! And this above all: Treasure your loved ones and hold them close. Let them know how much you care. And if you're as young as Bronny James or Damar Hamlin, I also say this: find your passion, find your calling, find the people and the work that will drive you, inspire you, and give real meaning and purpose to everything you do during your limited time on this planet.

Bronny and Damar bring us other golden lessons too: about how to handle life's inevitable setbacks and turn them into fuel for your inner fire. Soon after his crisis, Damar jumped right back into action with the Buffalo Bills, and he played well, so well that he was a candidate for the NFL's Comeback Player of The Year for 2023. Ultimately, the award went to Joe Flacco of the Cleveland Browns, but I'm sure Damar felt honored to be in the running. Bronny James bounced back too: soon after his heart defect was fixed, he was back on the court for USC, and playing so well that he is now playing for the L.A. Lakers, the team of his storied father. Wow!

Today, as I applaud Damar and Bronny for their courage and their resilience, I can hear the spirit of Nick Saban ringing in my ears, just as I described it earlier: "To reach the top, you have to have a special passion, a special intensity, a special focus, and always, always, always you have to have an iron-like commitment to keep right on learning and growing. And when trouble comes, and you suffer the inevitable setbacks and hardships that life will throw in your path, you don't quit. Ever! You dig in, you learn the necessary lessons, and then you stand up and charge right back into action, stronger, wiser, and even more determined to reach the top."

Yes! That's the spirit! That's what the great champions do! Just think of Tom Brady. Michael Jordan. Kobe Bryant. Steph Curry. Or LeBron James. And for me, Bronny's dad summed it up perfectly:

"Never underestimate the heart of a champion." ∎

48

Certified B Corporation

Now comes a story I cherish, and it all begins with Patagonia.

I love wearing Patagonia's jackets and vests, and I love Patagonia's commitment to quality, and its unflinching commitment to protecting our environment and our wilderness areas. Admirable! So of course I had to read all about Patagonia's founder, Yvon Chouinard. And Yvon wrote a book that I absolutely adore: *Let My People Go Surfing, The Education of A Reluctant Businessman*. For me, it's pure inspiration.

Yvon Chouinard was the son of a French Canadian blacksmith, and growing up he was an adventurer and sportsman who loved hiking and mountain climbing, who loved surfing and swimming and just being out in the wild, surrounded by everything that Mother Nature has bestowed upon us. With his passion for the outdoors, Yvon naturally became an ardent environmentalist and social activist and—as he states in the subtitle of his memoir—"A Reluctant Businessman." That said, his business smarts and his higher sense of purpose proved to be a winning combination.

From a quiet start in Ventura, California, back in 1973, Patagonia is today an international powerhouse, with an iconic brand, stores in more than 10 countries, and factories in 16 countries. Not bad for a "reluctant businessman!" Indeed, Patagonia stands today as a great American success story, and in his book Yvon introduced me to what I see as another great American success story now in the making: the Certified B Corporation.

The Certified B program is something unique in American business: a pioneering campaign committed to elevating a company's standards and performance in five key areas: 1.) How you treat your employees. 2.) How you treat your customers. 3.) How you serve your community. 4.) What you do to protect our environment and take care of our planet. 5.) And how you maintain the highest standards of corporate governance. In sum, those five categories measure a corporation's commitment to fulfill its business needs, yes, but to do so in a way that also serves a far greater good.

The Certified B initiative was launched by three idealistic MBA grads: Jay Coen Gilbert, Bart Houlahan, and Andrew Kassoy. After earning their MBAs at the Wharton School of Business, Jay and Bart co-founded a company called AND1, to produce a line of basketball shoes and clothing. And they designed AND1 to be a model of enlightened management and corporate governance. It featured shared company ownership, generous parental leave benefits, and annual contributions of 5 percent of company profits to worthy causes. From their many overseas suppliers, Jay and Bart demanded strong worker protections regarding wages, health care, and workplace safety. Admirable! And Jay and Bart drew their inspiration from some of the most revered names in American business: Patagonia, Ben & Jerry's, and the actor Paul Newman's enduring legacy, Newman's Best.

Alas, AND1 was not built to last. The company did well during the 1990s, and by 2001 it was reporting annual revenues of $250 million. But then its sales and profits slumped, and in 2005 Jay and Bart were forced to pivot: they sold AND1 and began looking for a more sustainable way to promote their idealistic causes. To do that, they joined forces with Andrew Kassoy, their former classmate at Wharton who was then working at a private equity firm, one also dedicated to promoting positive social change. It was a good fit, and the three of them soon launched "B Lab," a non-profit platform for their ambitious Certified B campaign. And their ultimate goal was both bold and laudable: to generate a global movement in support of using advanced business skills and power to help build a far better world.

Yvon Chouinard set the hook, and thanks to some further reading I came to a stunning realization: the ideals and values that the Certified B program was promoting are very much in line with the ideals and values that my family embraces and that we have woven deep into the fabric of The Republic of Tea and our River Road Family Vineyards and Winery. So right there I became determined to join the movement and earn Certified B status for our young River Road Family Vineyards and Winery. I felt confident that joining the Certified B movement would help us become a stronger company and also a more powerful advocate for the greater good.

The process of B Certification is very demanding. On each of its five elements of corporate governance, B Lab experts evaluate your company's performance on a scale of 0 to 100. And in each category, to be approved you have to score an 80 or above. You also have to include in your bylaws a formal declaration pledging to use a portion of your profits for a worthy cause. And this is not a one-time certification. To maintain your status as a Certified B Corporation, you have to be re-evaluated and pass their test every three years. Before we started the process, our winery had already been certified by outside experts regarding how well we maintain the highest standards of sustainability and environmental protection in our vineyards and throughout our wine-making process. But the B Lab process and its governing standards pushed us to reach much higher.

We started the process in October of 2020, and we hired a very experienced consultant to help guide our way. It took us 651 days of hard work, heavy investment, and constant improvement, but in August of 2022 we did it: our winery earned the status of a Certified B Corporation. And with that we joined the ranks of Patagonia, Ben & Jerry's, Newman's Best, and a growing list of blue-ribbon companies, here and abroad, who are now members of the Certified B community. At that stage, we were one of only five wineries in California to achieve that status, five out of 4,000 wineries, and for us this was indeed a badge of honor and a cause for celebration.

Today, more than 9,161 companies have joined the Certified B movement, representing 162 industries and 102 different countries. At our winery we feature the Certified B seal of approval on our labels, on our website, and right on the front door of our winery. Our real joy, though, comes from something much deeper, from feeling a part of something new and important, a global effort to use business power for the greater good.

There is another element here too. As you have seen throughout these pages, starting with my dad and Uncle Julian, we as a family believe that entrepreneurs and business leaders have an obligation to use our talents and influence to promote positive social and cultural change, for the good of us all. Honor and Share! For me, that is the true significance of the Certified B movement, and we are immensely proud to be a part of it. ∎

49

Podcasts and ChatGPT

How far we've come.

When I was growing up, back in the 1950s and '60s, our telephones were big and clunky, with clumsy dials, and we got most of our news and sports from our local newspaper or radio stations. For major national and international news, we relied on our three national TV networks; back then that's all we had. And in the early years of TV, most of our shows came to us in black and white; the arrival of color was hailed as a revolution.

Growing up in Southern Illinois, I loved baseball, and I loved playing baseball, but my favorite teams were not the Cubs or the White Sox up in Chicago, or the St. Louis Cardinals, just to the west of us. No, my favorite team was the Dodgers, first when they were in Brooklyn, and later when they moved out to L.A. And game after game, year after year, my personal heroes were the Dodger greats: Duke Snider, Roy Campanella, and the greatest pitcher of that era, Sandy Koufax. If you wanted heroes to look up to, to inspire you, and to set you dreaming of reaching the very top of your own chosen field, the Dodgers were as good as it gets.

My wife Pam knew, of course, of my boyhood love of the Dodgers, and as I got older she did something special: she arranged for me to attend the Dodgers' spring training camp in Vero Beach, Florida. And this was not just to sit in the stands, watch a few games, and eat a few hotdogs. No. This was a Dodger program that took devoted fans right into the heart of the Dodger experience. To give us the full feel, they gave us a Dodger uniform to wear, coaches to instruct us, and they even gave us time out on the field to chase groundballs or shag flies in the outfield. And to top it all off, they gave each of us time in the batting cage, to face big league Dodger pitchers and see what we could do. Wow! Talk about a dream come true!

But guess what? In that batting cage, I instantly realized that I was way out of my league. I couldn't touch a fastball, and a big league curve left me diving for cover. Still, I loved every minute of it. And I still have a photo of me with Roy Campanella, both of us in uniform and me grinning like a kid. For me, that photo is the symbol of an era, a symbol of a time gone by.

Two decades later, something else momentous happened. One day a pal and I were chatting and he said, "Say, Ron, do you follow the Dodgers' podcasts?" Podcasts? At that point I had never even heard the word! But soon I was hooked. Right on my laptop, on my iPhone, in my car, or even out on a jog, I could listen to podcasts and follow my beloved Dodgers. Or get expert health and nutrition advice. Or insider views of the big news of the day. For me, this was a stunning development. If the arrival of color TV was hailed as a revolution, just consider what the iPhone, the Internet, email, text messaging, and podcasts are giving us today: The World, right at our fingertips—and enormous power to change it too. Think about it:

Every minute of every day, no matter where we are, thanks to our iPhone or like phones we have access to personal phone calls and messages and to millions and millions of news reports, books, movies, photos, and information from all around the globe. And should an earthquake hit, or a devastating fire, or a political crisis, often we can watch the drama unfold in real time. Likewise, in times of emergency, we can use our phones to notify our families or call for help, just as Dave Shrum did when his pal Steve collapsed with a heart attack. Yes, how far we've come—and how fast!

And now comes ChatGPT...

Now, I'm no techie. Far from it. But today I have ChatGPT right on my iPhone, and I can use it to brainstorm, draft memos, or help me write our Strategic Plans or polish our press releases. How to announce major news? ChatGPT can give me guidance and effective wording too. Likewise, if you're rushing into a meeting and need to make a major presentation, you have ChatGPT right there to help. Also, if you're suddenly feeling woozy and want to check your blood pressure, you can do that too right on your iPhone. Yes, tools of revolution, right in our hands! Tools, alas, that can be used to inform—or misinform. Tools that can be used to foment hatred and division—or, in better hands, to work for the greater good.

What an exciting time this is! What an exciting time to be a young entrepreneur or business leader! And if you need a healthy jolt of energy and inspiration, just consider what one man was able to do: Steve Jobs.

Steve Jobs was born in 1955, and he grew up in Los Altos, in the heart of what is now Silicon Valley. As a boy, Jobs was a misfit at school, but he loved tinkering with electronics, and at the ripe old age of 12 he needed a few parts for a frequency counter he was building. So what did Steve Jobs do? He picked up the phone and called Bill Hewlett, one of the brilliant founding partners of Hewlett-Packard, the high-tech pioneer.

Impressed, Bill Hewlett gave the kid the parts he needed—plus a summer job working on an electronics assembly line.

So at the age of 12, Steve Jobs was passionate and off and running on ambitious projects. After high school, Jobs went to Reed College, up in Portland, but again classical schoolwork bored him and after one semester he dropped out. He felt that what he was learning didn't justify what it was costing his parents to send him to Reed. But Jobs stayed on campus, sitting in on a few classes and sleeping on the floor of friends' dorm rooms. But then Steve Jobs found a subject that really set him on fire: Calligraphy. How words can be stylishly created and put onto the page—or onto a screen! And right there a dream—and soon a revolution!—was born.

Soon Jobs found a pal, a pal with a passion for designing electronic devices: Steve Wozniak. The two young men set up shop in Steve Jobs' family garage, and on April 1st, 1976, they launched a little venture called Apple, with what is now an iconic visual hammer: a stylish apple with a bite out of its side. And soon something else came out of that garage: a quirky looking little box, the first Mac computer. What the heck is this, people wondered? And what can it really do?

Well, here we are, just a half century later, and Apple has changed our world. Profoundly. Mac desktops and laptops—and like computers and compatible tools from Microsoft, HP, Dell, Toshiba and countless other companies—are now essential tools of modern life in America and in countries throughout the world. Today, in nearly every home, school, and office in America we have Macs and other computers equipped with an array of applications to educate us, train us, enlighten us, and turn the harshest of tasks and the craziest of ideas into dazzling realities. Then came Apple's iPad—so much power, in such a slender packet—and then in June of 2007—*drumroll, please!*—Apple brought forth the first iPhone, with all its ingenious, life-enhancing tools hidden inside. Yes, powerful tools of revolution, right in our hands. Over the past

50 years, Apple has produced and sold millions of computers, and millions of iPads, and it has distributed millions of songs via iTunes. Great! But guess what? Since 2007, Apple has manufactured and sold *billions* of iPhones. Yes, *billions*. Tools of revolution, in billions of hands all around the globe. Wow! Fabulous!

Yes, how far we've come. Early on, Steve Jobs, that college dropout blessed with extraordinary passion and talents, vowed "to put a ding in the universe." And he succeeded far beyond anyone's imagination. Indeed, Jobs and his legions of fellow entrepreneurs, creators and business leaders have put incredible tools in our hands, and they have helped all of us forge our own exciting Roads to Greatness. For me, the lessons here are clear: Be Bold! Dream Big Dreams! Innovate! Educate! Honor and Share! And as you build, learn the lessons and embrace the exciting can-do spirit of Steve Jobs, Sam Walton, Yvon Chouinard, Bill Campbell, Nick Saban and so many others, the spirit that programs *We can do it! Yes we can!* ▪

50

Write A Book

Let me repeat those uplifting words: *We can do it! Yes we can!*

In writing this book, and drawing together the wisdom and guidance I gleaned from my own business experience and from reading so many books about great leaders and business pioneers, those words were always right there with me, cheering me on. How did the legendary coach Nick Saban lead his college football teams to seven national championships? He created for them a culture of success, instilling deep in each of his players and coaches the determination, the mindset, and the unshakable conviction that, yes, we can reach the very top of the football world. *Yes we can!*

How did Sam Walton, growing up on poor farms in Oklahoma and Missouri, rise to the very top of the business world? By working his tail off and doing exactly what my dad urged me to do: Learn, Learn, Learn! And how did a young guy like me, growing up in Southern Illinois, wind up building successful businesses in the distant worlds of premium tea and fine wine? By learning, by growing, and by taking some exciting leaps and risks. Be bold! Innovate! Educate! Honor and Share! *We can do it! Yes we can!*

Always key too, was my Lesson No. 1: Find a mentor. Find men and women who can guide and inspire you every step of the way. People like Al Ries. Barbara Shomaker. Tripp Frohlichstein. The teams at YPO. And that was especially true when I ventured out into the world of wine. When I first came out to California to study grape-growing and wine-making, back in 1971, there were only two dozen wineries in Napa Valley and even fewer in Sonoma County. Worse, there were very few people here in America who believed that we as a nation could ever produce fine wines that could stand proudly beside the very best of France, Italy, Germany or Spain.

Still, there were a handful of true believers—leaders and winemakers like Robert Mondavi, Warren Winiarski and Mike Grgich, among others—and they led the way. And they were convinced that with vision, hard work, bold innovation, and an unshakable can-do spirit we could indeed become a leader in the world of fine wine. And guess what? Today the wines of Napa Valley and Sonoma County are celebrated throughout the world, and that's just the beginning. Today we are making quality wines in every single state in our union—all 50 of them! Imagine that! *We can do it! Yes we can!*

As I see it, that same resilient, unshakable can-do spirit is now at the heart of the Certified B movement, as it tries to use the power of business to build a better, more far-sighted world. And that same can-do spirit is at the heart of our Trained for Saving Lives campaign, with our goal of training wineries and other businesses and equipping them with life-saving AEDs. Can we really save countless lives every single year? *Yes we can!*

Now, my friends, as our journey together draws to a close, there is one final lesson I want to highlight for you, and it is a lesson very dear to my heart: Write A Book! Computers, satellites, and iPhones are fabulous tools, of course, but books are fabulous tools as well, and they are tools of enduring power and value. As you have seen throughout these pages, when you are in need of wisdom, guidance or inspiration, there is nothing that can beat a quality book, especially a book written by the masters of their chosen craft. Just think back to what we all have learned from Nick Saban, Sally Jenkins, Al Ries, Bill Campbell, John Bogle, Sam Walton, Yvon Chouinard and many others too—so much wisdom, so much rock-solid, hands-on advice about how to properly manage your business and your life, and about how to turn your most cherished dreams into shining realities.

And just consider this: none of the books we have discussed here was written yesterday; indeed, several were written 30, 40 or even 50 years ago! Timeless jewels. And the wisdom, spirit, and guidance they bring us today is still fresh and relevant, and they will probably be fresh and relevant for our children and grandchildren too. Now that's power! That's value! And that's why, for so many centuries, quality books have been cherished pillars of our culture and our civilization, helping to guide and inspire us along our way.

As you saw, one book upended my entire life: *The Republic of Tea, How An Idea Becomes A Business*. When I read it, Pam and I were living a quiet life in Southern Illinois, life was good, but that book set me on fire. The setting was San Francisco, challenge and excitement were in the air, and that book set me off on an adventure that would change the future of our lives and our family, and also the lives and families of the thousands of people who, over the years, joined our companies and built their own successful lives and dreams in the process. Who could ask for more? So I often bow in gratitude to Mel and Patricia Ziegler, for writing that book and sending me happily down my own special Road to Greatness. Hoo-rah!

Still, as I built our companies and traveled the world to do it, I did have one question rattling around inside my head: what about writing your own book? Can writing your own book help you develop as a leader? Can writing a book help build your business? In sum, I wondered, is writing your own book really worth all the time, effort and commitment it takes?

In search of answers, one day I sat down with my pal Mel Ziegler. After all, Mel and his wife Patricia and their friend Bill Rosenzweig wrote *The Republic of Tea*, and they had made it a shining success. So with Mel I cut right to the heart of it: "Tell me, Mel, was that book good for your business? Are you happy you did it?" Mel just laughed and said, "Ron, yes! Writing a book is the best PR move you can make for any start-up company!"

As Mel explained, writing that book helped them crystallize their thinking, it gave them a deep sense of meaning and purpose, and when the book came out, Mel, Patricia and Bill all promoted it with book signings and special events, and the result was a PR bonanza. I was impressed. Deeply. Then one day Thomas Newmark, a pal of mine in St. Louis, came to me with a vexing problem. He had launched a company selling vitamins and natural cures for disease, and his company was struggling. So I said to him, "Tom, you know what you should do? Write a book!"

Tom was surprised, but he took my advice and joined forces with a master herbalist named Paul Schulick. The result was *Beyond Aspirin, Nature's Answer to Arthritis, Cancer & Alzheimer's Disease*. The book sold well, and it generated positive reviews in *The Wall Street Journal* and *The New York Times*—PR gold!—and Tom and Paul did radio interviews and garnered attention throughout the worlds of health and natural medicine. Tom was thrilled, of course, and it certainly helped build his business!

If I needed any further convincing, I got it from Mel and Patricia Ziegler. After they sold The Republic of Tea to me, what did they do? They sat down and wrote another delightful book, *Wild Company, The Untold Story of Banana Republic*. Again, the result was a PR bonanza, and it certainly enhanced the success and the reputation of their prized first baby, the Banana Republic. Mel and Patricia were thrilled, of course.

That said, when I decided to write this book, my intent was not to use it as a PR tool, or as a way to boost sales at The Republic of Tea or our River Road Family Vineyards and Winery. No. I wrote it to inspire. I wrote it to touch hearts and light fires. I wrote it to share with you, my readers, the many lessons I have learned during my 70-plus years on this planet. And I wrote it with the hope that my own experience might inspire each of you to follow your hearts, build your dreams, and to always hold inside you, deep inside your being, those seven magical words: *We can do it! Yes we can!* That was my ultimate goal. And, in closing, I pray that I have succeeded.

With my very best wishes to each of you... ▪

—

A FINAL SALUTE

As you have seen throughout these pages, I had the good fortune to be guided and inspired by a remarkable group of men and women as I grappled with the many challenges of entrepreneurship and business leadership. Many of these men and women have passed on, but I hope their wisdom and spirit will now become permanent gold in your own backyards.

With that hope, I offer a final salute to my dad, Hyman A. Rubin, and to Julian B. Venezky, Frank Fourez, Jr., Al Ries, Tripp Frohlichstein, Dr. Robert Lefton, Barbara Lyons Stewart, Bob Bailey, Frank Nitikman and George Phillips, our cherished colleague at The Republic of Tea. Each of them brought me magnificent lessons, and may their light now shine brightly for each of you as well. ∎

GOLD IN YOUR BACKYARD

First Edition 2025

Published by Val de Grace Books, Napa, California

ISBN: 979-8-9858787-5-2

Library of Congress Control Number: 2024923330

Design by Connie Hwang Design

Printing by Artron Art Printing (HK) Ltd through Crash Paper

Photo credit: Todd Rubin